Prepare to Pass

BPTC Professional Ethics

2019-20

Third Edition

Gillian Woodworth

Prepare to Pass

BPTC Professional Ethics

2019-20

Third Edition

Gillian Woodworth

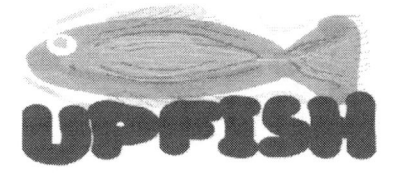

Upfish Business Services Ltd

2019

Copyright ©2019 by Gillian Woodworth

All rights reserved. This book or any portion thereof may not be reproduced or used in any manner whatsoever without the express written permission of the publisher except for the use of brief quotations in a book review or scholarly journal.

First Edition Printing: 2018

Second Edition Printing 2018

ISBN: 978-0-244-83050-2

Upfish Business Services Ltd
Park Street Lane
St Albans

Ordering Information:
Special discounts are available on quantity purchases by corporations, associations, educators, and others. For details, contact the publisher at gwoodworth.upfish.law@gmail.com

This book sets forth a system for answering the centrally assessed assessment in Professional Ethics. It is based on the syllabus as it stands for the 2020 assessments. The ethos behind it is to suggest answering techniques which are relevant for the assessment in this current form. This book majors in suggested techniques for answering questions featuring Part 1 of the syllabus through the use of incremental learning. It features activities to include in your learning and in your revision together with ways in which you can ensure that you have covered the whole of the syllabus by the time of your 2020 assessment.

The author

Gillian Woodworth transferred from full-time professional practice to working in full-time legal education in 1995. Since then she has spent over 24 years training students on both academic and professional legal courses and as a regulator of those courses. She worked for 10 years at BPP as a tutor, as Course Director and as Director of Staff Training and Development; she has worked as a visiting lecturer at what is now the University of Law; she then worked in the Education and Training department of the Solicitors Regulation Authority prior to moving to what is now The City Law School, City University of London.

Gillian worked for over 6 years full-time at City, teaching and assessing initially on the on the Bar Vocational Course and latterly on the BPTC course where she also had a responsibility for ensuring The City Law School's compliance with Bar Standards Board requirements.

In addition to writing and marking final assessments for LLB, GDL, LPC, BVC and BPTC programmes and supervising dissertations at LLM level, Gillian has also trained professional legal course external examiners. She is therefore well placed to provide advice and guidance on how to pass assessments at all levels of legal education.

In 2017 she joined the Bar Standards Board marking team for Professional Ethics, marking both the spring and autumn sits of the assessment.

By the same author

The Sixth Edition of **"BPTC Revision: Prepare to Pass Civil Litigation 2019-2020"** should be available for the spring and summer 2020 sits after the end of November 2019.

Feedback

This feedback is reproduced with the kind permission of each of the individuals who provided it.

2019

- *I wanted to tell you that I passed Professional Ethics and I could not have done it without you. It was my second sit and I am so glad I don't have to do it ever again. It would not have been possible without you*

    A BPP student

- *I am just emailing you to let you know that I've passed and indeed your book did help me understand a lot of things, thus I'd like to thank you very much for all the help through your book.*

    A UWE student

- *THANK YOU SO MUCH I COULDN'T HAVE DONE IT WITHOUT YOU!*

    A BPP student

- *I just wanted to thank you for all your help and the amazing exam technique I learnt from you.*

    A City student

- *One thing I often lacked is confidence. Thanks to you I feel great. The latest edition of your book is indeed great. Thank you so much.*

    A BPP student

- *Thank you for your amazing help.*

- *I managed to get a VC. Thank you.*

August to November 2018

- *Your teaching session and your book were instrumental in passing Ethics in August. Thank you so much. (A student from CLS).*

- *Your book was invaluable. I just kept your technique in mind when I felt flustered. Thank you for my VC! (A student from UOL, London)*

- *Thank you for your book. I really think your guide to answering took me over the hill. I went from a 56 to a 75, crazy. (A student from UOL, Birmingham).*

April to July 2018

- *Our teaching session was brilliant. (A student from CLS).*

- *What I learned from Gillian was question answering techniques - which applies to any ethics question - how to get maximum points for your information/knowledge. (A student from UWE).*

- *Thank you for an excellent session. (A student from CLS).*

- *"I was tutored by Gillian in both Professional Ethics and Civil Litigation. In every lesson, I found Gillian's style and approach very helpful and well structured. Her assiduous focus on mock exam questions and exam technique in general is priceless in terms of breaking down how to approach two of the toughest modules on the BPTC. Similarly Gillian's* Prepare to pass Civil

Litigation *book is very useful as unlike other civil litigation books, it corresponds exactly with the BSB syllabus and content" (A student from UOL, London).*

- *Yesterday I got my ethics results – a high competent - BIG BIG surprise! It means I have been awarded marks for everything I wrote down. A few of my schoolmates have managed to finish all 6 questions but still failed. I think your strategy works for me! Thank you so much, and I hope my Provider could adopt the way in which you taught me at the start of the course! (A student from CLS).*

Thank you from the author

Thank you to those students from

- BPP
- The City Law School City University of London,
- The University of Law and
- the University of the West of England

who kindly assisted in the preparation for this book,

….. and thank *you* for buying this book.

Any feedback to help enhance next year's edition will be gratefully received. Please email gwoodworth.upfish.law@gmail.com

I hope that this book helps you on your way towards an enjoyable and successful career at the Bar or as a lawyer in your home jurisdiction.

Gillian Woodworth

Assessment dates for the 2019-2020 BPTC

All centralised assessments start at 2pm

Professional Ethics Monday 6th April 2020

You 10 clear days in between the Professional Ethics Assessment and the Civil Litigation and Evidence Assessment on 17th April 2020, although that includes the Easter weekend; and then a weekend before the Criminal Assessment on 20th April 2020.

Professional Ethics Monday 17th August 2020

Please do note that if you are sitting more than one centrally set assessment in the summer sitting of the BPTC assessments

that all 3 assessments take place in the same week, on Monday, Wednesday and Friday of the week beginning 17th August, with Professional Ethics first, then Civil Litigation and Evidence, then Criminal Litigation.

Format of the Assessment

The assessment is 2.5 hours long. It is closed book: i.e. you must understand and learn the entire contents of the syllabus. The examination is centrally set by the Bar Standards Board Central Examination Board, so that all candidates sit the same paper. It is marked by human beings.

There are 6 Short Answer Questions. More detail on the format of both questions and answers follows in this book.

Introduction

CONTENTS

Feedback			ii
Assessment dates			vi
Introduction			1
FIRST "HALF"	Planning how to structure your answer		3
		Student reports	5
		Before you start (1)	11
		Format of Questions	17
		Format of Answers	21
		The Rubric Planning Template (1)	23
		The Big Reveal	29
		The Rubric Planning Template (2)	30
		The Rubric Planning Template	31
		Question A	33
		Beginning to plan the answer to Question A	34
		The syllabus	39
		Before you start (2)	45
		Using the syllabus to build the answer to Question A (1)	45
		Once you have finished this book (1)	55
		Question A	56
		Using the syllabus to build the answer to Question A (2)	57
		Timing	83
		Guidance for Question A	105
		A possible mark scheme for Question A	113
SECOND "HALF"	Selecting the contents of your answer from the syllabus		119
		THE CONDUCT RULES	121
		YOU AND THE COURT *Rules* and *CORE DUTIES*	121
		BEHAVING ETHICALLY *Rules* and *CORE DUTIES*	126
		YOU AND YOUR CLIENT *Rules* and *Core Duties*	129
		Guidance on *CORE DUTIES*	137
		YOU AND THE COURT *Guidance*	139

Introduction

		YOU AND THE COURT *Rules, CORE DUTIES* and *Guidance* all on one page	141
		BEHAVING ETHICALLY *Guidance*	145
		BEHAVING ETHICALLY *Rules, CORE DUTIES* and *Guidance* all on one page	149
		YOU AND YOUR CLIENT *Guidance first page*	151
		YOU AND YOUR CLIENT *Rules, CORE DUTIES* and *Guidance first page* all on one page	155
		YOU AND YOUR CLIENT *Guidance second page*	158
		YOU AND YOUR CLIENT *Rules, CORE DUTIES* and *Guidance second page* all on one page	161
		YOU AND YOUR CLIENT *Guidance third page*	164
		YOU AND YOUR CLIENT *Rules, CORE DUTIES* and *Guidance third page* all on one page	167
		YOU AND YOUR CLIENT *Guidance fourth page*	170
		YOU AND YOUR CLIENT *Rules, CORE DUTIES* and *Guidance fourth page* all on one page	173
		Once you have finished this book (2)	175
	And Finally		
		Question N	177
		Themes	179
		Think like an examiner (1)	183
		Once you have finished this book (3)	185
		Answering Question N (a)	187
		A possible mark scheme for Question N (a)	201
		Think like an examiner (2)	203
		The final form Rubric Planning Template for this book	205
		Answering Question N (b)	207
		A possible mark scheme for Question N (b)	211
		What if?	212

Introduction

After stepping back from full time employment when I officially retired, students whom I tutored privately for the civil litigation assessment began to report that the ethics assessment was a particularly difficult one to pass. Given my life - long interest in all aspects of assessment and my accumulated expertise in the assessments for the Bar Course (from the Bar Conversion Course, through to the Bar Vocational Course and now the Bar Professional Training Course), I was curious enough to want to investigate this for myself. I also hope to help BPTC candidates along the way.

Thus, having marked and set questions for the BPTC Civil Litigation assessments since the course began, I joined the marking team for the BPTC Professional Ethics papers for both the spring and summer sits in 2017.

As with my "Prepare to Pass" BPTC Civil Litigation book, you will find that this Professional Ethics book employs Activities for you the learner to carry out. This is one way of encouraging you to engage with the subject matter. You need to become so familiar with Professional Ethics, so conversant with it, in an engaged way, to the extent that in addition to spotting the issues and citing the relevant ethical rules, you can also properly apply those rules to the ethical issues arising in the assessment scenarios and then finally suggest ethical solutions to them; and sometimes practical solutions as well.

It may seem a little odd to have to learn these ethical rules for a closed book assessment when once in pupillage and beyond you will be able to check the rules by looking them up. I suspect that the aim of this mode of assessment is to ensure that once in pupillage and beyond, you will have a gut reaction and a natural instinct as to when an ethical issue that is a problem has arisen or may arise. Then you will know where to go to check out the way to handle it and will therefore make the right ethical decisions. That said, my understanding is that from 2020 there is to be a centrally assessed open book second limb to Professional Ethics, undertaken during pupillage, following a first limb assessment set by the Providers of the course.

For the time being, then, The BPTC Professional Ethics assessment is not the kind of assessment where you can learn a template that works for different 'topics' on the syllabus. Professional Ethics are a fact of everyday life as a legal professional. The variety of different scenarios that come up in the assessment are as many and as varied as there are situations in life. Imagine being an agony aunt or uncle in a popular publication. They cannot give the same piece of advice, learned from a template, for problem "x". There are too many varying factors.

It is intended that working through this book will give you an insight into what is needed to pass the assessment in its current form. For that reason you also need to be aware from the outset that this book is not intended to contain the detail of the whole of the syllabus. Rather it will give suggestions for ways to study in order to become extremely familiar with the content of this assessment, together with suggested question answering techniques.

Do please note from the contents pages of this book that there are two headings in this book called "Before you start". It is well worth looking at those pages before you start, so that you can have the basic preparations done before you start to study or revise in earnest.

Introduction

This is a book of two "Halves".

THE FIRST "HALF"

Planning how to structure your answer

The First "Half" takes you through a technique which ensures that your approach to writing your answer is one which includes those points for which there is credit on the mark scheme.

In order to achieve this you will be walked through planning how to structure an answer to a Professional Ethics question.

Therefore, in the First "Half" of this book you will be told which elements of the syllabus need to be referenced in your answer.

THE SECOND "HALF"

Selecting the contents of your answer from the syllabus

The Second "Half" of this book reinforces the incremental learning technique which is introduced in the First "Half" of the book, suggesting that you consider adopting and adapting it as one way to become fully conversant with the contents of the whole syllabus.

Gillian Woodworth

November 2019

THE FIRST "HALF"

PLANNING
HOW TO STRUCTURE
YOUR ANSWER

The First "Half"
Intentionally Blank

Student Reports

What students had reported to me about the Professional Ethics assessment pre-2017 and the beginnings of suggested solutions

We will discover the in-depth solutions to these points when working through how to plan and present your answers.

I. "I had learned the Handbook and the other parts of the syllabus by heart and yet I still didn't pass."

Initial Suggested Solution

Read the question, answer the question.

II. "This is the first assessment I have ever failed in my life. How can that be? How come my tried and tested assessment technique failed me this time?"

Initial Suggested Solution

Read the question, answer the question. Take on board what the rubric[1] of the assessment says that examiners and markers are looking for.

III. "The assessment must be fundamentally flawed."

Initial Suggested Solution

I feel that learning **and applying** this fundamental element of the BPTC is something that can only be done over the course of time and with lots of practice. Learning the syllabus verbatim will just not cut it. You need to develop a feel for the approach to any one of the infinite number of ethical issues there are, in tandem with correctly identifying which elements of the syllabus are relevant to the situation about which you are advising.

IV. "When I look at the suggested answers for the BSB mock assessments, I do seem to know it all, it looks familiar; it just seems as though I am not writing down the things that marks are given for. How can I be sure to identify the parts of the Handbook/syllabus that attract the marks on the mark scheme – it's a forest of similar words and phrases."

Initial Suggested Solution

The specifically taught element of the Professional Ethics course is relatively short. In this book there are suggested techniques for identifying the parts of the syllabus to use in your answer. This technique will take time to acquire but it is a necessary part of preparation for being successful in this assessment.

V. "There is not enough time in the assessment to fully complete my answers. I simply did not have time to finish the paper. I only answered 4 and a half out of the 6 questions."

Initial Suggested Solution

From what I have been told, even when you can correctly identify the parts of the syllabus being tested, there appears to be just about enough time available to write out an answer, with little or no time for planning so that some (most? / all?) candidates just write without planning. This leads to some answers meandering and they are sometimes not on point and / or do not evidence a logical train of thought. This results in candidates not actually answering the question. This book suggests a technique to address this. Practising the

---

[1] The contents of the rubric will be dealt with in the sections called "Format of Questions" and "Format of Answers"

technique over and over before the assessment may help candidates to become very familiar with the syllabus content and so provide higher calibre answers.[2]

> **Activity**
>
> **Take some time now to search your favourite internet search engine for**
>
> **'Flash Anzan'**
>
> **and /or**
>
> **'Saroban'**
>
> **along with**
>
> **'world championships'**

Notice how very small children enjoy the game of mental arithmetic which they invariably get right. Notice how by adulthood the best in the world can give the correct answer to the addition of around 15 different 3 – digit numbers in way under 2 seconds, and all in their head. It is not only impressive, but also possible.

In a similar way you need to be able to identify ethical issues, work mentally through the contents of the Professional Ethics syllabus, extract the correct elements, then plan your answer to apply the elements to the scenario and then write your answer, all within 25 minutes for every 10 marks available in the assessment.

Timing is an issue for many in this assessment. To me as a marker it was unclear whether students were in fact planning their answers or whether they were aware of how short time is and ploughed headlong into what they think is the best answer they can give in this time pressured environment.

Perhaps precious time is 'wasted' when candidates cite several or all lines of a particular rule when it is in reality only the first (or fourth, or whichever,) sub paragraph of a rule that is relevant to the answer. Learn to trust yourself to set out just the bit of any long rule that is relevant to the question. Also remember that it is only the Core Duties that must be cited verbatim. Other elements of the syllabus can be paraphrased.

From the hundreds of questions I marked, which I believe included some from every provider, not one script ever followed exactly or was even a close approximation of the mark scheme. That is totally fine and totally to be expected. What gave me pause for thought was the relatively high number of candidates who did not manage to answer the question.

VI. "I've heard that if the marks on the paper indicate a question is worth 5 marks then I should be sure to write down 10 things as there are often half marks rather than whole marks on

---

[2] One of my students, having answered only 4 and a half questions on the spring 2018 sit, achieved a good pass - although I am told this was not their intended strategy! *Please* take heed of the section in this book on Timing.

the mark scheme. Yet I still don't seem to be writing down the 10 things they are looking for."

Suggested Solution

Yes, to a point I can see where you are coming from. On the 2017 assessments I found there were plenty of marks available on the mark scheme, adding up to quite a few more than the maximum amount of marks available; so that raises the question of why some students are not picking up these marks. I think in part this was attributable to candidates not fully answering the questions as they did not always adhere to the assessment rubric[3]. For instance, a question could ask, "What should you do and what should you say to your solicitor" Weaker answers would deal with only one of these questions.

VII. "My feedback said that I did not apply the facts to the rules and so I did not gain marks"

Suggested Solution

Students often feel that they have answered the question fully, that they can say no more. During the marking process I often felt that candidates would have left the assessment thinking they had done well as it was obvious that they had dutifully and diligently committed large parts of the syllabus to memory and had written them out in their answers. Even so, what they had not done was fully answer the questions.

By using this book you will learn to ensure that what is in your head actually gets onto the script to be marked, and appreciate that what may seem to you to be repetition is in fact the way to gain marks for application.

VIII. "What if I did a full answer to a question, but the parts of the syllabus I used are not on the mark scheme?"

Suggested Solution

You will have learned my response to that by the end of this book.

Next a couple of points on poor techniques to be avoided when answering questions in the assessment.

Poor techniques to be avoided

i. If a candidate sets out all the Core Duties, either at the beginning of their script or at the beginning of each answer, that alone will gain no marks. Such candidates are expecting markers to telepathically refer back to the right one at the right time. No, we will not do that!

Suggested Solution

Markers can only mark what we see on the scripts. To gain the marks available candidates need to actively engage the assessment rubric[4] in their answers.

In doing so, that means that a good framework for an answer to any Professional Ethics question can be drafted before you have even seen the question! [5]

---

[3] The contents of the rubric will be dealt with in sections called "Format of Questions" and "Format of Answers"
[4] ditto
[5] In a few pages time you will meet the Rubric Planning Template which throws more light onto this.

ii   An example of a poor answer that, sadly, on the 2017 scripts I marked, was not particularly rare, is roughly as follows.

Question - "Person A said x to Person B. Person B subsequently did y." What are the ethical issues that arise? How would you resolve them?

Very poor answer - "A barrister must act with honesty and integrity". Then the weaker candidates would go on to quote [irrelevant things] verbatim.

<u>Suggested Solution</u>

Remember that apart from the Core Duties, which must be quoted verbatim, the rest of the syllabus you are allowed to paraphrase in your answers.

Clearly, away from the assessment environment, you can agree that this very poor answer does not answer the question as there has been no application to the facts and no answer to the question of how to resolve the ethical issues.

The next section of this book works through one particular question, demonstrating how to approach questions, analyse them and answer them. At the end of this process as well as being in the position to tackle any question posed in the assessment, you should also be able to 'write your own' ethics questions following the system explained throughout this book. In the end, you may be thinking like an examiner![6]

---

[6] More on this in the Second "Half" of this book.

Intentionally Blank

What you can usefully do either before you start the professional ethics course, or at the start of your revision.

The approach of most students I have spoken to has been to read, re-read, re- re-read and re-re-re-read the Handbook and the remainder of the syllabus in the hope that it will eventually sink in. If that approach works for you, all well and good. If not, or even if you are just curious, read on!

Trying to learn Professional Ethics without actually being in practice as a Barrister could be likened to learning to drive a car without actually getting in one. Apologies to those of you who have yet to learn to drive – it's all very well to learn by heart that to stop a car you remove your right foot from the accelerator onto the brake and almost simultaneously depress the clutch with your left foot. Being able to repeat that in a written assessment does not mean that you will perfectly execute an emergency stop the first time that you are behind the wheel. Your current lack of practical experience as a Barrister could hinder you in the assessment, in its current form, especially when coupled with assessment nerves. Things will become much clearer when you've experienced practice as a Barrister. Yet you still need to pass this assessment first! Do not despair, however. Engage brain and common sense in the assessment alongside what you have learned by heart. Hopefully then you will not do something as ridiculous as responding that you would return the brief on which you have been working for months, shortly before trial, when that is clearly not an appropriate course of action, having put together the facts of the scenario and the relevant ethical rules.

Having said that, there are sections of the Handbook that it would serve you well to rote learn **now** as they are lists that feed into many of the answers to questions I have seen.

In the Handbook these are, in my opinion

- Part 2 section B – **THE CORE DUTIES** – sometimes referred to as simply CDs. These must be learned VERBATIM for the assessment;

- The 10 elements in rC21 on **[not]** *Accepting Instructions* in Part 2 Section C3, the Conduct Rules in the YOU AND YOUR CLIENT section of the Handbook. These do not need to learned verbatim; they can be paraphrased in your assessment answers; and

- The 10 elements listed in gC96 as being included as *serious misconduct* In Part 2 Section C4, the Conduct Rules in the YOU AND YOUR REGULATOR section of the Handbook; they can be paraphrased in your assessment answers.

With this in mind you are strongly recommended to carry out the following 3 activities now.

Before you start (1)

Activity

The 10 CORE DUTIES to learn verbatim are

Activity

The 10 elements on *when not to accept instructions* **are (paraphrased)**

Before you start (1)

Activity

10 examples of *serious misconduct* are (paraphrased)

Before you start (1)

If, in order to complete the 3 activities above, you used the online colour coded version of the Handbook, you will have noticed that

- the outcomes (O) are coloured in orange;
- the rules (rC) are coloured in red; and
- the guidance to those rules (gC) are coloured in green.

The first drafts of this book were also colour coded in the same way, with additional layers if colour coding to aid your learning. Sadly, this pushed up the costs of printing to prohibitive heights.

Therefore, this book uses different fonts rather than different colours.

For now, simply be aware that

- *references to rCs in the Handbook are written in this font, Cambria Math, pitch 11, bold and italicised.*

- ***any relevant guidance (gC) in the Handbook are written in this font, Broadway, pitch 11, bold and italicised.***

It is thus suggested that you take some time, every few pages as you work through the book, to highlight this book in the relevant colour coding, if that would help your personal style of learning.

- *So this should be red to correlate with the rCs in the Handbook*

- ***and this should be green, to correlate with the Guidance to the rCs in the Handbook.***

Until you reach the end of Rubrik Planning Template (1) [see the headers on each page], the footnotes will set out the font and colour for you; after that you should be able to continue with the colour coding yourself, should you wish to.

The eagle-eyed amongst you may have wondered about the strange fonts appearing in the contents pages and activity boxes of this book. Now you know why they are like that!

You could now add to your colour coding repertoire the fact that in this book *THE CORE DUTIES, WHICH ARE SET OUT IN PART 2 SECTION B OF THE HANDBOOK, ARE WRITTEN IN THIS FONT, ALGERIAN, PITCH 11, BOLD AND ITALICISED. THERE IS NO COLOUR ASSIGNED TO THE CORE DUTIES IN THE HANDBOOK, SO YOU CAN PICK YOUR OWN COLOUR AND WE'LL CALL THIS COLOUR 3* (where red was colour 1, and green was colour 2, say).

Intentionally Blank

Content and Format of Short Answer Questions in the Professional Ethics assessment

All 6 questions are allotted 10 marks.

For each question there is usually a short scenario, then question a). (say 5 marks)

Next the scenario is embellished, then question b). (say 5 marks)

Here are 4 examples of the way that parts a) and b) have been known to be phrased.

> Question A
>
> By reference to the applicable Core Duties and other principles of the Handbook, which ethical issues arise from [this scenario] and how should you resolve them?
>
> Question B
>
> Identifying the ethical principles that arise and how they apply to this scenario, explain what you are permitted to do with regard to [...] and how you should respond to [...]
>
> Question C
>
> What should you do next in respect of [....] and what are the ethical principles that should inform your actions in this situation?
>
> Question D
>
> With reference to the applicable Core Duties and other principles of the Handbook, describe the ethical issues that arise in this scenario for your lay client and for you and what action, if any, she or you should take as a result.

At this point I am going to state the obvious; please bear with me as many students' assessment answers do not obviously do what I am about to suggest.

You could divide your script into separate sub paragraphs, taken from the question itself, each with a suitable space in between for your answer *(once you have planned it)*. This at least should guarantee that you do answer the question as it is posed. For instance

Answer to Question A

The applicable Core Duties

The other applicable principles of the Handbook

How I should resolve them

Answer to Question B

The ethical principles

1. xxxxxxxxxxxxxxxxxxxx

How this applies

2. yyyyyyyyyyyyyyyyyyy

How this applies

What I am permitted to do with regard to […]

How I should respond to […]

… and similarly for Questions C and D.

Even so, this approach may not lead to you gaining all the marks you feel you deserve.

The missing link is that this approach does not address the assessment rubric. You may not have heard of this term. THE ASSESSMENT RUBRIC IS CRUCIAL. IT IS WHAT THE EXAMINERS ARE LOOKING FOR. YOU WILL NOT MAXIMISE YOUR MARKS IF YOU DO NOT MAKE USE OF IT. It sets out what the examiners are looking for in assessment answers. Where you are supposed to access it from, in order to adhere to it in your answers, is explained on the next page. I just feel that not many students in 2017 took it on board.

Format of Questions

The Assessment Rubric

You need to think of the elements of the assessment rubric as forming part of the question as it is posed.

Your Provider will no doubt provide you with copies of the assessment rubric during your course; it will likely be set out, as it has been every year so far, at the front of your BSB provided mock assessment, as well as at the front of your actual assessment.

I am of the opinion that many candidates often do not take note of this rubric when answering questions, based upon the scripts I marked in 2017. That is something that can be easily remedied by working through this book.

Content of the rubric for the Professional Ethics Assessment

Listed here are some elements of what may be included in the rubric for your assessment again this year. The contents of it should not be ignored. Below are what the author considers to be those parts of the rubric which a large number of students do not appear to have heeded when writing their assessment answers.

- *Do not limit yourself to make the same number of points as the marks available.*

- *You will not be required to quote the relevant paragraph number(s) in the Handbook or other source material. However, you are expected to quote accurately the Core Duties that are applicable in any sub-part of a question.*

- *This exam is intended as a test of your ability to identify the ethical issues engaged in the questions*

- *and then to apply your knowledge of Professional Ethics*

- *in seeking to resolve those issues.*

The next section of this book deconstructs the assessment rubric in a way that should help you to write answers that should attract the marks that are on the mark scheme.

Intentionally Blank

Content and Format of your Short Answers in the Professional Ethics assessment

Before deconstructing the rubric, you will find it helpful to know that in broad outline - detail is to come later – the syllabus is made up of 4 parts, henceforth in this book to be known as the 4 AREAS of the syllabus.[7]

Area 1 is the examinable parts of the Handbook; this contains the Code of Conduct, *CORE DUTIES*, the Conduct Rules - outcomes, *rules* and *guidance* on those rules; similarly, the rules applying to particular groups of regulated persons; scope of practice; practising certificate rules; and CPD rules.

Area 2 is Code Guidance, Guidance on the Administration of a Barrister's Practice, Guidance on the Professional Conduct of Barristers, Additional Guidance;

Area 3 is Crown Prosecution Service Publications; and

Area 4 is Money Laundering and terrorist financing.

Each Area is NOT tested separately. Any given question can require the content of the relevant sections of one, more or all 4 areas of the syllabus.

For the purposes of this book alone, Areas 2, 3 and 4 of the syllabus are dealt with as one entity and typed in *Elephant, pitch 11, bold and italicised, (colour 4)*.

Deconstructing the content of the rubric

Listed here again, from the end of the Format of Questions section of this book, are those elements of what may be included in the rubric for your assessment again this year if it stays the same as in previous years – the elements which the author considers to be the most important parts to note *and respond with* when framing your answers in the assessment are highlighted as follows.

(The standard type face is the actual rubric, **THE UPPER CASE BOLD WORDS** have been so **HIGHLIGHTED BY THE AUTHOR**; those word *italicised in bold* have been *added in by the author*).

- Do not limit yourself to make the same number of points as the marks available.
  - *so there are half marks available;*
  - *perhaps also sometimes two elements need to be included in your answer to gain a half mark;*
  - *sometimes there is a whole mark available or none at all;*
  - *chief examiners do spend time when drafting the mark scheme to ensure that what they consider is a fair weighting is given to points to made by candidates; i.e. those points which will attract half a mark and those which will attract a whole mark;*
  - *some mark schemes allow marks or half marks for including in the answer an "issue" that is not a problem, so that there are marks available for saying, e.g. that the barrister has done x, that this is perfectly acceptable as the Handbook states that barristers can do x, there has therefore been no breach of the ethical rules and so the barrister does not need to report any serious misconduct.*

---

[7] To avoid confusion between the 4 parts of the syllabus and then the parts that part 2 of the syllabus is divided into (!) I am referring to the 4 parts of the syllabus as the 4 areas of the syllabus.

- You will not be required to quote the relevant paragraph number(s) in the Handbook or other source material. However, you are expected to quote accurately the *CORE DUTIES* that are applicable in any sub-part of a question.

   Where the author has included the relevant paragraph numbers in this book it is purely to help you navigate through the subject content. The CORE DUTIES you will have to learn verbatim.

- This exam is intended as a test of your ability to **IDENTIFY THE ETHICAL ISSUES** engaged in the questions

To help with your assimilation of this skill I am introducing a system of different fonts.

(i)

- *state each ethical issue generically* [8] and

(ii)

- set out the relevant rules (rC) in the Handbook (Part 1 in the syllabus – the Bar Standards Board Handbook) [9];

- *DIRECTLY CITE THE RELEVANT CORE DUTIES* [10];

- *paraphrase of any relevant guidance (gC) in the Handbook* [11]; and

- *refer to any relevant parts of those elements numbered 2-4 in the syllabus* [12]

- and then to

(iii) [13]

- *APPLY YOUR KNOWLEDGE of Professional Ethics*
- *by referring to the actual facts in the scenario and*
- *stating whether or not there has been /would be a breach of a barrister's professional ethics*

- in seeking to

(iv) [14]

- *RESOLVE THOSE ISSUES*
- *by stating what should be done/not done.*

---

[8] Colour 5 *Lucida Calligraphy*; after red, green, colour3 and colour 4.
[9] red
[10] Colour 3
[11] green
[12] Colour 4
[13] Colour 5 – *Lucida Calligraphy*
[14] Colour 6 – *Segoe Script*

Format of Answers

You should please note that numbers (i) and (iii) both use the same font as they are linked to each other. This is because (i) is a statement of the issue in general terms and (iii) is the application of your knowledge of the issue by reference to the facts of the scenario.

This is distilled into template form on this and on the next page, where the four points above now form the headings of the 4 columns of the template. We will call this Rubric Planning Template. You will later use this template to create your own Rubric Planning Template for each sub – question.

By the time you get to revision stage and the actual assessment, it is anticipated that the Rubric Planning Template will be reduced to a few squiggles and hieroglyphs that only you can interpret, as it will need to be done in as short a space of time as possible.

We are now, though, starting to go through the stages of slowly building up the Rubric Planning Template, which by assessment time you will reproduce in full in a flash when planning your answers.

(i) Identify ethical issues. State them generically [15]	(ii) set out the relevant bits of the syllabus i.e.
	• **Syllabus Part 1;**
	  ○ Relevant parts of the Handbook –
	  ○ Part 1, 2[16], 3, 4 or 6?
	  ○ **Equality Rules?**[17]
	• *any of syllabus Parts 2, 3 and 4?* [18]
		(iii) apply your knowledge with a reasoned explanation of breach/no breach [19]	(iv) Resolve i.e. advise [20]

---

[15] Colour 5
[16] Part 2 of the Handbook contains *CORE DUTIES*, rules of conduct (rC), *guidance on those rules (rG)*.
[17] You will need new colours for each of Parts 3, 4 and 6 of the Handbook and the Equality Rules.
[18] Colour 4
[19] Colour 5
[20] Colour 6

The Rubric Planning Template (1)

To help you remember the headings of each column, you could devise for yourself an acronym that works for you. My students had the **IDEA** for the following acronym and slotted it onto the top of the Rubric Planning Template:-

Identify the Issue	*Describe the relevant parts of the syllabus*	*Explain with reference to the contents of the scenario*	*Advise resolve*

(i) Identify ethical issues. State them generically [21]	(ii) set out the relevant bits of the syllabus i.e.
	• Syllabus Part 1;
	  ○ Relevant parts of the Handbook –
	  ○ Part 1, 2 [22], 3, 4 or 6?
	  ○ Equality Rules? [23]
	• *any of syllabus Parts 2, 3 and 4?* [24]
		(iii) apply your knowledge with a reasoned explanation of breach/no breach [25]	(iv) Resolve i.e. advise [26]

In order to help you learn how to piece together your answers in this assessment, we are going to work in detail through a question, Question A, (you will get the full substance of the question in a few pages time), which needs in its answer references to

- Syllabus Area 1 (which is the Handbook),
  ○ Part 2 of the Handbook (which is the Code of Conduct),
    ▪ Part B of the Code of Conduct (which is the Core Duties)
      • and some elements of Part C (which is the Conduct Rules).
        ○ The relevant parts of Part C are
          ▪ Part C1 (which is YOU AND THE COURT),
            • Part C2 (which is BEHAVING ETHICALLY) and
              ○ Part C3 (which is YOU AND YOUR CLIENT).

This part of the syllabus has been frequently tested in past assessments.

At this point, remember that you are simply taking it from me that the Question requires the contents listed above in your answer. In the "Second "Half" of this book, we will look at suggestions as to how to arrive at that yourself. It is the contents listed above that you will use to build up the contents of column (ii) of the Rubric Planning Template.

---

[21] Colour 5

[22] Part 2 of the Handbook contains *CORE DUTIES*, rules of conduct (rC), *guidance on those rules (rG).*

[23] You will need new colours for each of Parts 3, 4 and 6 of the Handbook and the Equality Rules.

[24] Colour 4

[25] Colour 5

[26] Colour 6

The Rubric Planning Template (1)

We are now taking it that we have identified the content above that our Question A engages. Therefore, note how in the version of the Rubric Planning Template below, column (ii) has been contracted down to only that.

Identify the Issue	**D**escribe the relevant parts of the syllabus	**E**xplain with reference to the contents of the scenario	*Advise* *resolve*

(i) Identify ethical issues. State them generically [27]	(ii) set out the relevant bits of the syllabus i.e.
	• RELEVANT CDS [28]
	• Conduct rules (rC)
	  ○ YOU AND THE COURT
	  ○ BEHAVING ETHICALLY
	  ○ YOU AND YOUR CLIENT [29]
	• *relevant guidelines (gC)* [30]
		(iii) apply your knowledge with a reasoned explanation of breach/no breach	*(iv) Resolve i.e. advise*

This is the blank	second row of the template	referred to	below.
First ethical issue	CD 1 [31]		

Next, you need to know that this book follows a pattern of incremental learning where, for now, you

— first learn the relevant CORE DUTIES [32] (You have already done this in one of the earlier Activities);

— secondly, practise and learn the *Conduct Rules* [33] i.e. the outline headings beginning with YOU AND THE COURT [34] through to YOU AND YOUR PRACTICE; [35]

— thirdly, practise and learn *the contents of each of those subheadings* [36], before you

— fourthly, practise and learn *the guidance to the contents of each of those subheadings and how they relate to* [37] the individual conduct rules [38].

---

[27] Colour 5
[28] Colour 3
[29] red
[30] green
[31] Colour 3
[32] Colour 3
[33] red
[34] red
[35] red
[36] red
[37] green
[38] red

The Rubric Planning Template (1)

Once you have all that under your belt, which you will have, for Question A, from our working through Question A together, it will then remain for you to decide whether or not it will suit your learning style to work through in the same way for the remainder of the syllabus.

From the above Rubric Planning Template for Question A, you can already plan the outline of an answer before you have read the scenario! The following example is for when only CD1 is engaged (although at assessment level and in real life it is likely that more elements of the syllabus will also be engaged.)

The first ethical issue is [..........]. [39]

THIS ENGAGES CORE DUTY 1 WHICH STATES [CITE IT VERBATIM]. [40]

In this scenario [state what is actually happening that engages the part of the syllabus you have just set out, here [41]*, CORE DUTY 1* [42]*]. Doing this will [or will not] be a breach of CD1 because [..........].* [43]

To resolve this I would / would not [...........] and I would [tell my lay client / solicitor that [what will happen next]. [44]

We are now going to show how writing your assessment answers in the above format means that you actually do answer the question as written, yet more importantly, you also include all 4 elements of the Rubric Planning Template in your answer. This is demonstrated by mapping the forms of questions onto the Rubric Planning Template. Here again are our Questions A – D. In the assessment you will plan your answer by inserting the exact wording of the question as it is written, into the blank second row of the Rubric Planning Template above. Here is how to do it.

Question A

By reference to the applicable Core Duties and other principles of the Handbook, which ethical issues arise from [this scenario] and how should you resolve them?

Question B

Identifying the ethical principles that arise and how they apply to this scenario, explain what you are permitted to do with regard to […] and how you should respond to […]

Question C

What should you do next in respect of [….] and what are the ethical principles that should inform your actions in this situation?

Question D

With reference to the applicable Core Duties and other principles of the Handbook, describe the ethical issues that arise in this scenario for your lay client and for you and what action, if any, she or you should take as a result.

---

[39] Colour 5
[40] Colour 3
[41] Colour 5
[42] Colour 3
[43] Colour 5
[44] Colour 6

The Rubric Planning Template (1)

The first 3 rows are the headings we have so far used for columns (i) (ii) (iii) and (iv).

The next 3 rows show the start of planning an answer to Question A.

The rows on the page after that show the start of planning an answer to Questions B, C and D.

Identify the Issue	**D**escribe the relevant parts of the syllabus	**E**xplain with reference to the contents of the scenario	*Advise resolve*

(i) Identify ethical issues. State them generically [45]	(ii) set out the relevant bits of the syllabus i.e.
	• Syllabus Area 1;
	  ○ Relevant parts of the Handbook –
	  ○ Part 1, 2 [46], 3, 4 or 6?
	  ○ Equality Rules? [47]
	any of syllabus Areas 2, 3 and 4? [48]
		(iii) apply your knowledge with a reasoned explanation of breach/no breach [49]	(iv) Resolve i.e. advise [50]

(i) Identify ethical issues. State them generically [51]	(ii) set out the relevant bits of the syllabus i.e.
	• *RELEVANT CDS* [52]
	• *Conduct rules (rC)*
	  ○ YOU AND THE COURT
	  ○ BEHAVING ETHICALLY
	  ○ YOU AND YOUR CLIENT [53]
	• *relevant guidelines (gC)* [54]
		(iii) apply your knowledge with a reasoned explanation of breach/no breach	(iv) Resolve i.e. advise

Question A			
which ethical issues arise from [this scenario]	By reference to the applicable Core Duties and other principles of the Handbook		and how should you resolve them
First ethical issue	CD 1		

---

[45] Colour 5

[46] Part 2 of the Handbook contains *CORE DUTIES*, rules of conduct (rC), *guidance on those rules (rG)*.

[47] You will need new colours for each of Parts 3, 4 and 6 of the Handbook and the Equality Rules.

[48] Colour 4

[49] Colour 5

[50] Colour 6

[51] Colour 5

[52] Colour 3

[53] red

[54] green

The Rubric Planning Template (1)

Question B			
Identifying the ethical principles that arise	Identifying the ethical principles that arise	and how they apply to this scenario	explain what you are permitted to do with regard to [...] and how you should respond to [...]
Question C			
	and what are the ethical principles that should inform your actions in this situation		What should you do next in respect of [...]
Question D			
describe the ethical issues that arise in this scenario for your lay client and for you	With reference to the applicable Core Duties and other principles of the Handbook		and what action, if any, she or you should take as a result

Things to notice

Questions A, C and D – sometimes questions do not seem to fully cover the rubric, but this does not mean that you have answered the question fully if for these 3 questions you do not include in your answer columns (i) and (iii) of the Rubric Planning Template. YOU MUST INCLUDE ALL FOUR COLUMNS OF THE RUBRIC PLANNING TEMPLATE TO GET GOOD MARKS EVEN IF IT IS NOT OVERTLY MENTIONED IN THE QUESTION FORMAT.

Question D - Notice that the question asks 'for your lay client and for you'. You therefore need to have separate parts of your answer for each of these two people.

Question B - The best phrased questions mirror the rubric, thus prompting candidates to answer as per the four columns in the Rubric Planning Template.

Even if the question were to ask you only to spot the ethical issues, you should still fill out your answer with something in each of the four columns of the Rubrik Planning Template.

On the next page is the big reveal. It is what, from my marking of the Professional Ethics assessments in 2017, I think many, many students failed to do when sitting this assessment.

It is
COLUMNS III) AND IV)
of the
Rubric Planning Template that candidates do not seem to include in their answers!!!!!!!

The Rubric Planning Template (2)

However, we are not yet at the point in the creation of a full Rubric Planning Template to be completing **columns (iii) and (iv)**. I do hope, though, that you are already remembering that those elements **need to be in your answer too**, in addition to columns (i) and (ii) which previous candidates did seem able to address in their answers.

We are now going to start to answer Question A (even though we have not yet seen the scenario!) We are starting out, as before with the premise that the scenario engages *CD1*.

Now we are going to shift the approach we have so far adopted to filling in column (ii). Remember that we said the worst assessment technique ever is where students list out all the *CORE DUTIES* at the beginning of their answer paper and then perhaps expect markers to refer back to them for each question. Markers will not do that. In any event, such a list will not be producing any application as it does not include the use of column (iii) of the Rubric Planning Template.

ONE LIST AT THE BEGINNING OF YOUR ANSWER PAPER ATTRACTS NO MARKS.

Filling in column (ii) of the Rubric Planning Template

You should already have learned the *CORE DUTIES* by heart.

Even though they appear before the *Conduct Rules* in the Handbook, the best method my students found for dealing with the *CORE DUTIES* in assessment answers is **not to use the *CORE DUTIES* as a starting point to your answer.** Rather, it works really well when you map them onto your understanding of the Handbook/rest of the syllabus. This method makes it much easier to identify the *CORE DUTIES* that are actually relevant to your answer.

For example, by the time the assessment comes, you will have learned that the first section of the *Conduct Rules* in the Handbook is called *YOU AND THE COURT*.

The first section of the rules in *YOU AND THE COURT* deals with *a duty to the court to act with independence in the interests of justice*. (This is the beginning of *rC3*).

If you have identified that your *duty to the court to act with independence in the interests of justice* is relevant to your answer, then the use of the words *'duty to court..... independence in the interests of justice'* should spark in your memory not only *CD1* – *"YOU MUST OBSERVE YOUR DUTY TO THE COURT IN THE ADMINISTRATION OF JUSTICE"* but also *CD4* - *"YOU MUST MAINTAIN YOUR INDEPENDENCE"*.

Thus your answer to the question should contain reference in column (ii) of the Rubric Planning Template to

- the rule in the Handbook which sets out that barristers have a *duty to the court to act with INDEPENDENCE IN THE INTERESTS OF JUSTICE* AND TO
- *CD1* AND to
- *CD4*

For this reason I train students to map the *CDS* into their answer planning AFTER they have identified the relevant *rules (rC) of the Handbook* and BEFORE they add in *relevant guidelines (gC)* and any of the Equality Rules and then *any of syllabus areas 2, 3 and 4* into the Rubric Planning Template column (ii).

The Rubric Planning Template

Here is that information put into an extract of the now revised Rubric Planning Template which we used for Question A.

Notice that this question gives an overt reminder that there are other principles in the Handbook as well as *CORE DUTIES* that should inform your answer. Even though it does not appear to ask for the contents of column (iii) of the Rubric Planning Template, YOU DO STILL NEED TO INCLUDE THIS IN YOUR ANSWER.

(i) *Identify ethical issues. State them generically*	(ii) **set out the relevant bits of the syllabus** **For Question A,** • *Conduct rules (rC)* *YOU AND THE COURT* *BEHAVING ETHICALLY* *YOU AND YOUR CLIENT* • *RELEVANT CDS* [55] • *relevant guidance (gC)*	(iii) *apply your knowledge with a reasoned explanation of breach/no breach*	(iv) *Resolve i.e. advise*
Question A			
which ethical issues arise from [this scenario]	By reference to the applicable Core Duties and other principles of the Handbook		and how should you resolve them
First ethical issue	YOU AND THE COURT • duty to the court to act with independence in the interests of justice • CD1 • CD4	• *[to be filled in]* • *[to be filled in]* • *[to be filled in]*	• *[To be filled in]* • *[To be filled in]* • *[To be filled in]*
	BEHAVING ETHICALLY (if relevant – broken down in the same way across the columns)		
	YOU AND YOUR CLIENT (if relevant – broken down in the same way across the columns)		

---

[55] NOTICE THE CHANGE TO THIS NEW, PERMANENT ORDER OF *Rules first, CDS SECOND*.

The Rubric Planning Template

Then continue in column (ii) for all the relevant sections of the Handbook for the first ethical issue.

Please do remember that at this stage, due to learning the syllabus incrementally, we are dealing ONLY with the *Conduct Rules* and *CORE DUTIES*. In the assessment you will in addition be adding in the relevant *guidance*, which we will do later in this book for Question A.

Then you can plan in a similar way for each of the ethical issues you have identified.

Here, now, is the scenario for Question A.

Question A

Today is Tuesday. You are spending today preparing for a court appearance as Counsel tomorrow. On Thursday and Friday your professional diary states that you are spending those days preparing for a two - day court appearance as Counsel on Monday and Tuesday next week. Your best friend has just telephoned to say that he/she has booked a long weekend for you both in Prague on a flight leaving at 6.30 am this Thursday and returning in the afternoon on Sunday. He/she tells you that they have booked lots of tours and entertainment, so don't expect a minute to yourself! You privately tell your clerk you would like to go as it is your friend's birthday. Next time you are in the reception area of Chambers, where there are solicitors and lay clients waiting to meet with other barristers, your clerk tells you that she has seen other barristers who in similar situations have done their preparation on the plane rather than miss out on a holiday and says that you should do the same. When you later ask her more about that, she says it was a long time ago in different chambers and they are all probably retired by now.

By reference to the applicable Core Duties and other principles of the Handbook, which ethical issues arise from this scenario and how should you resolve them

(i) Identify ethical issues. State them generically	(ii) set out the relevant bits of the syllabus For Question A • RELEVANT CDS • Conduct rules (rC) YOU AND THE COURT BEHAVING ETHICALLY YOU AND YOUR CLIENT • relevant guidance (gC)	(iii) apply your knowledge with a reasoned explanation of breach/no breach	(iv) Resolve i.e. advise
Question A			
which ethical issues arise from [this scenario]	By reference to the applicable Core Duties and other principles of the Handbook		and how should you resolve them
Not preparing fully for court	YOU AND THE COURT • duty to the court to act with independence in the interests of justice • CD1	• Clerk suggests I prepare on the plane. Must make my own decisions and not blindly depend on clerk's advice preparing on the plane would be in breach of this duty because I had given myself 2 full days to prepare; it will likely be rushed and not to the best of my abilities. It would not	• [To be filled in] • [To be filled in]

33

Beginning to plan the answer to Question A

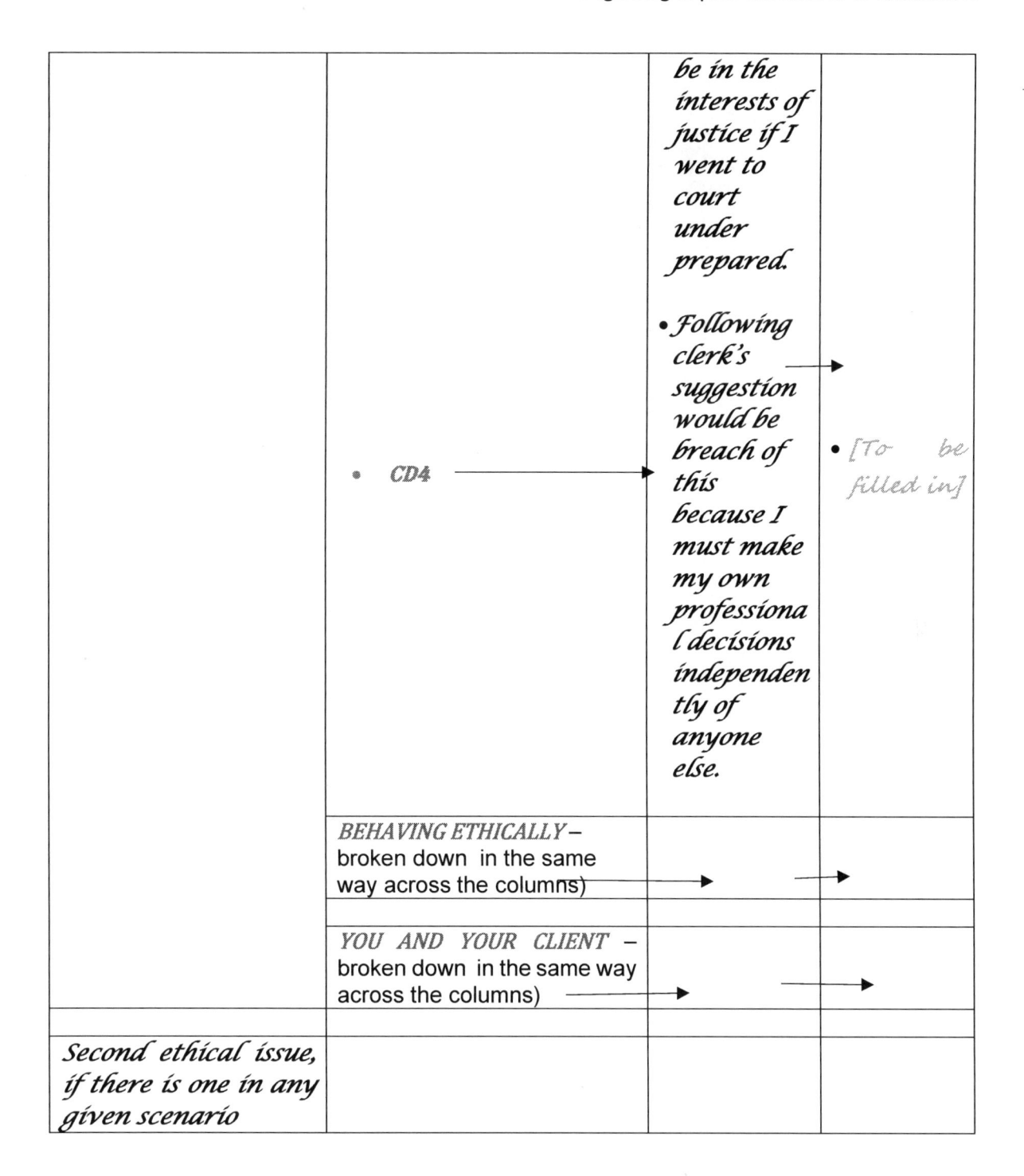

	• CD4	be in the interests of justice if I went to court under prepared. • Following clerk's suggestion would be breach of this because I must make my own professional decisions independently of anyone else.	• [To be filled in]
	BEHAVING ETHICALLY – broken down in the same way across the columns) →	→	
	YOU AND YOUR CLIENT – broken down in the same way across the columns) →	→	
Second ethical issue, if there is one in any given scenario			

There are more elements needed to be added to columns (ii) and (iii) for a very full answer to our Question A (i.e. *the guidance*). We will add this in when we get to that *guidance* section later in this book.

Next, you will need to add in the contents of column (iv).

(i) Identify ethical issues. State them generically	(ii) set out the relevant bits of the syllabus **For Question A** • *RELEVANT CDS* • Conduct rules (rC) YOU AND THE COURT BEHAVING ETHICALLY YOU AND YOUR CLIENT • *relevant guidance (gC)*	(iii) apply your knowledge with a reasoned explanation of breach/no breach	(iv) Resolve i.e. advise
Question A			
which ethical issues arise from [this scenario]	By reference to the applicable Core Duties and other principles of the Handbook		and how should you resolve them
Not preparing fully for court	YOU AND THE COURT • duty to the court to act with independence in the interests of justice • CD1	• Clerk suggests I prepare on the plane. Must make my own decisions and not blindly depend on clerk's advice preparing on the plane would be in breach of this duty because I had given myself 2 full days to prepare; it will likely be rushed and not to	• I will make my own decision about whether or not to plan on the plane. • I will not prepare on the plane, I will take the 2 days I originally felt I needed to plan or

35

Beginning to plan the answer to Question A

		the best of my abilities. It would not be in the interests of justice if I went to court under prepared.	the 2 day court appearance next week.
	• CD4 →	• Following clerk's suggestion would be breach of this because I must make my own professional decisions independently of anyone else.	I will tell my friend that my professional duties and ethical principles mean that I cannot go on the trip to Prague this weekend.
	BEHAVING ETHICALLY – broken down in the same way across the columns) →	→	→
	YOU AND YOUR CLIENT – broken down in the same way across the columns) →	→	→
Second ethical issue, if there is one in any given scenario			

36

Beginning to plan the answer to Question A

So your answer to Question A as it stands at the moment (before further bits of the Handbook are added to it later on to make it a fuller answer) could look something like this.

The first ethical issue which arises is potentially not preparing fully for a court appearance.

— *There is a rule in the YOU AND THE COURT SECTION OF THE Handbook to the effect that barristers have a duty to the court to act with independence in the interests of justice.*

My clerk suggests I prepare for next week's court appearance on the plane to and from Prague so that I can go there this weekend. I must make my own decisions and not blindly depend on my clerk's advice.

I will resolve this issue [56] by making my own decision about whether or not to plan on the plane.

— *ALL BARRISTERS ARE BOUND BY 10 CORE DUTIES (CDS). CD1 IS RELEVANT HERE. IT STATES THAT, "YOU MUST OBSERVE YOUR DUTY TO THE COURT IN THE ADMINISTRATION OF JUSTICE."*

Preparing on the plane would be in breach of this duty because I had given myself 2 full days to prepare; it will likely be rushed and not to the best of my abilities if I were to try to do it on the plane. It would not be in the interests of the administration of justice if I went to court under prepared.

I will resolve [57] this issue by not preparing on the plane. I will take the 2 days I originally felt I needed to plan for the 2 day court appearance next week.

— *CD4 IS ALSO ENGAGED. IT STATES THAT, "YOU MUST MAINTAIN YOUR INDEPENDENCE".* [58]

Following my clerk's suggestion would be breach of CD4 because I must make my own professional decisions independently of anyone else.

I will further resolve this issue by telling my friend that my professional duties and ethical principles mean that I cannot go on the trip to Prague this weekend. I will take Thursday and Friday this week to plan fully that I originally deemed I need.

The second ethical issue which arises is……

---

[57] Note how the wording of the question has been used in the answer. This will show the marker that you are answering the question. You do not have to pick up the wording of the question, although it will look good if you do!

[58] Note how the *CORE DUTIES* are obviously quoted verbatim [as required by the rubric] with the use of quotation marks. These quotation marks are not necessary, although it will look good if you do use them!

Before we go on to work further on the answer to Question A, now is an opportune time to introduce the full syllabus, to help us do so. This we will need to enable us to fully plan the contents of column (ii) of the Rubric Planning Template.

The Syllabus

From this point on we will be using the Rubric Planning Template to create your own Rubric Planning Template for each question. You will create the latter from the former. You will answer the questions, filling in column (ii) using the syllabus content.

You have already seen that the syllabus is made up of 4 Areas:-

— Area 1 is the examinable parts of the Handbook. *CDS*, *rules*, *guidance* and more are in here;

— *Area 2* [59] is Code Guidance, Guidance on the Administration of a Barrister's Practice, Guidance on the Professional Conduct of Barristers, Additional Guidance;

— *Area 3* [60] is Crown Prosecution Service Publications; and

— *Area 4* [61] is Money Laundering and terrorist financing

---

[59] For the purposes of this book, these 3 are in Colour 4.
[60] For the purposes of this book, these 3 are in Colour 4.
[61] For the purposes of this book, these 3 are in Colour 4.

Full syllabus content

Beginning on the next page is the complete syllabus as taken from the Bar Standards Board website. **The bold initial statements, i.e. those that are preceded by a long hyphen below, are those paraphrased by the author as above.** *The italics are the syllabus quoted verbatim from the Bar Standards Board website.*

The syllabus

"The SAQs for all Ethics assessments in 2020 will be drawn from the following source material (NB. When sections of the Handbook are referred to, the material included is all rules and guidance within those sections.):

— **Area 1 is the examinable parts of the Handbook; this contains, in Part 2 of the Handbook the outcomes, CORE DUTIES, *conduct rules* and *guidance* on those rules and more. Parts 3, 4 and 6 of the Handbook and the Equality Rules are on the next page.**

1. **The Bar Standards Board Handbook – 4th edition updated July 2019 (Version 4.1) [as published on the BSB website]**

    Part 1

        A-D

    Part 2

        A

        B [62]

        C1, *conduct rules* and *guidance*

        C2. *conduct rules* and *guidance*

        C3 *conduct rules* and *guidance* [63][excluding rC31-rC63 inclusive],

        C4,

        C5.1 & C5.2

        D1.1 (rC99-rC105),

        D2.1 & D2.2

        D4

        D6

    Part 3

        B2, B3, B7 & B9

        C1 & C2

    Part 4

        B8

        C – rQ130-135

    [None of Part 5]

---

[62] Covered in this book when answering questions in this book
[63] Covered in this book when answering questions in this book

Part 6

The definitions section will not be discretely examined, but knowledge of the Handbook's definitions relevant to the rest of the syllabus is required.

Bar Standards Board Handbook Equality Rules

Sections 1 & 2

— *Area 2* [64] of the syllabus is Code Guidance

2. **Code Guidance**
    - ➢ *Guidance on Practising Rules and Requirements*
        - o Guidance for Unregistered Barristers (Barristers without Practising Certificates) - Supplying Legal Services and Holding Out
        - o Guidance for Barristers Supervising Immigration Advisers (Oct 2018)
        - o The Public Access Scheme Guidance for Barristers (Revised Feb 2018)
        - o 'cab-rank' Rule Guidance
        - o Guidance on Conducting Litigation - Sept 2017

    - ➢ *Guidance on the Administration of a Barrister's Practice*
        - o First Tier Complaints Handling (Revised May 2018)
        - o Guidance on Referral and Marketing Arrangements for Barristers Permitted by the BSB
        - o Confidentiality Guidance
        - o Guidance on Self-Employed Practice

    - ➢ *Guidance on the Professional Conduct of Barristers*
        - o Guidance on Reporting Serious Misconduct of Others
        - o Media Comment Guidance
        - o Guidance on Insurance and Limitation of Liability
        - o Guidance on Clash of Hearing Dates (Listings)
        - o Guidance on use of social media (Feb 17)

    - ➢ *Additional Guidance*
        - o Guidance on the Transparency Rules
            - o Introduction to the guidance
            - o Mandatory transparency rules for all self-employed barristers, chambers and BSB entities
            - o Additional transparency rules for those undertaking Public Access work

        - o Regulatory requirements for barristers – practising certificates (https://www.barstandardsboard.org.uk/regulatory-requirements/forbarristers/practising-certificate/

        - o Guidance on Practising Certificates for Pupils and Newly Qualified Barristers

---

[64] Colour 4

— *Area 3* [65] **of the syllabus is Crown Prosecution Service Publications.**

   3. **Crown Prosecution Service Publications**
      The Code for Crown Prosecutors – October 2018 (8th Edition)
      The Farquharson Guidelines –Role of the Prosecuting Advocates

— *Part 4* [66] **of the syllabus is Money Laundering and terrorist financing.**

   4. **Money Laundering and terrorist financing**
      http://www.barcouncilethics.co.uk/wpcontent/uploads/2017/10/aml_1st_version_guidance_may.pdf

      IN OUTLINE ONLY – based on the Executive Summary (paragraphs 1 to 35) of the Bar Council's Money Laundering and Terrorist Financing practice note.

---

[65] Colour 4
[66] Colour 4

The syllabus

It is well worth getting yourself a version of the Handbook that you have trimmed down to take out those elements of it that are not examinable this year. It is good advice to focus on what is actually on the syllabus.

Using the syllabus to build the answer to question A (1)

Using the syllabus to build the answer to question A (1)

We are now going to deconstruct this syllabus and then reassemble it by dint of incremental learning.

The order of the examinable parts of the Handbook is as follows. It is worth setting it out here as the Big Picture often gets lost when you are new to this, you become embroiled in the minutiae of the syllabus and then you perhaps panic or can't see the wood for the trees because this is an important professional assessment.

The Handbook is listed as the first Part of the 4 Parts of the syllabus. We will therefore start with that. You will add the other 3 Parts of the syllabus (i.e. *Parts 2, 3 and 4* [67]) into your learning later.

You are strongly recommended not to just skim these next few pages of lists in this book. Getting the structure of the syllabus and the framework of professional ethics is vital if you are going to correctly analyse the assessment questions and identify which are the relevant parts of the syllabus to any particular question or part of a question. By taking the time to properly assimilate the shape of the ethical rules at this early stage you will be doing yourself a huge favour.

AREA 1 OF THE SYLLABUS

— The Handbook

- **[Part 1 Introduction]**

- **Part 2 The Code of Conduct**

- **Part 3 Scope of Practice**

- **Part 4 The CPD rules**

- **[Part 6 Definitions]**

    Bar Standards Board Handbook Equality Rules
    https://www.barstandardsboard.co.uk/media/1665979/bsb_equality_rules_for_bsb_authorised_bodies_2015.pdf Sections 1 & 2

Part 1 of the Handbook does not seem to be tested.

---

[67] Colour 4

Using the syllabus to build the answer to question A (1)

Parts 2, 3 and 4 of the Handbook as just set out above will now be further broken down incrementally.

[Part 1 Introduction]

Part 2 The Code of Conduct

- A. Application
- B. *THE CORE DUTIES*
- C. *The Conduct Rules (rC); [remembering also (gC)]*
- D. Rules applying to particular groups of regulated persons

The Bar Standards Board Handbook Equality Rules

Part 3 Scope of Practice

- B2[68] - Provision of *reserved* legal activities and of legal services
- B3 - Scope of practice as a self - employed barrister
- B7 - Scope of Practice as an employed barrister (non - authorised body)
- B9 - Legal Advice Centres

- Practising Certificate Rules
  - C1 - Eligibility for practising certificates and litigation extensions
  - C2 - Applications for practising certificates and litigation extensions by barristers and registered European lawyers

Part 4 Qualification Rules

- Bar Training Rules
  - B8 – Conduct of students

- The CPD Rules
  - The mandatory continuing professional development requirements

[Part 6 Definitions]

---

[68] You do not need to learn this lettering and numbering. It is included here solely to indicate where in the syllabus they appear.

Using the syllabus to build the answer to question A (1)

Next we are beginning the job of adding even more flesh to the bones of Parts 2, 3 and 4 of the Handbook, breaking down each of Parts 2 to 4 of the Handbook in turn.

Part 2 - The Code of Conduct

A. Application – read through it to get the idea of what this contains.
B. *THE CORE DUTIES* – you have already noted these for yourself in an Activity and you should already be working on committing them to memory verbatim.
C. *The Conduct Rules (rC); [remembering also (gC)]*
D. Rules applying to particular groups of regulated persons

The next thing to break down is section C – *The Conduct Rules (rC); [remembering also that you will do (gC) later]*

Section C - The Conduct Rules [69]

C1 [70] *- YOU AND THE COURT*

C2 - BEHAVING ETHICALLY

C3 - YOU AND YOUR CLIENT

C4 - YOU AND YOUR REGULATOR

C5 - YOU AND YOUR PRACTICE

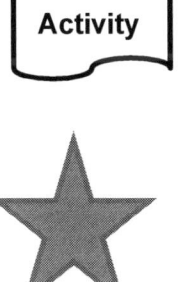

Activity

Learn these 5 main headings in the section on

Conduct Rules

NOW

so that you recite them in your sleep.

The next thing to break down is section D – Rules applying to particular groups of regulated persons.

---

[69] Red
[70] You do not need to learn this lettering and numbering. It is included here solely to indicate where in the syllabus they appear.

Using the syllabus to build the answer to question A (1)

<u>Section D - Rules applying to particular groups of regulated persons.</u>

D1[71] - SELF-EMPLOYED BARRISTERS, CHAMBERS AND BSB ENTITIES

D2 - BARRISTERS UNDERTAKING PUBLIC ACCESS AND LICENSED ACCESS WORK

D4 - UNREGISTERED BARRISTERS

D6 - PRICE AND SERVICE TRANSPARENCY RULES FOR SELF-EMPLOYED BARRISTERS, CHAMBERS AND BSB ENTITIES

Activity

**Learn these 4 main headings

in the section on

<u>particular groups of regulated persons</u>

NOW

so that you recite them in your sleep.**

---

[71] You do not need to learn this lettering and numbering. It is included here solely to indicate where in the syllabus they appear.

Using the syllabus to build the answer to question A (1)

The next thing to do in relation to Area 1 of the syllabus, the Handbook, is further break down the 5 main headings of the Conduct Rules; then the 3 main headings of the rules applying to particular groups of regulated persons.

The Conduct Rules

C1 [72] - YOU AND THE COURT

- *Independence in the interests of justice*
- *Not misleading the court*
- *Not abusing your role as an advocate*

C2 - BEHAVING ETHICALLY

- *Honesty, integrity and independence*
- *Referral fees*
- *Undertakings*
- *Discrimination*
- *Foreign work*

C3 - YOU AND YOUR CLIENT

- *Best interests of each client, provision of a competent standard of work and confidentiality*
- *Not misleading potential clients*
- *Personal responsibility*
- *Accepting Instructions*
- *Defining terms or basis on which instructions are accepted*
- *Returning instructions*
- *Requirement not to discriminate*
- *The 'cab-rank' rule*

C4 - YOU AND YOUR REGULATOR

- *Provision of information to the Bar Standards Board*
- *Duty to report certain matters to the Bar Standards Board*
- *Reporting serious misconduct by others*
- *Access to premises*
- *Co-operation with the Legal Ombudsman*
- *Ceasing to Practice*

C5 - YOU AND YOUR PRACTICE

- *Client money*
- *Insurance*
- *Associations with others*
- *Outsourcing*
- *Administration and conduct of self-employed practice*

---

[72] You do not need to learn this lettering and numbering. It is included here solely to indicate where in the syllabus they appear.

Using the syllabus to build the answer to question A (1)

> **Activity**
>
> Learn the above sections and bullet points
>
> of the
>
> <u>Conduct Rules</u>
>
> **NOW**
>
> so that you recite them in your sleep.

Using the syllabus to build the answer to question A (1)

> **Activity**
>
> The next thing for YOU to do is further break down the 4 main headings of the rules applying to
>
> <u>**particular groups of regulated persons**</u>
>
> in the same way that we did above for the conduct rules.
>
> There is room for you to do this below.
>
> Please fill in the blanks.

Rules applying to particular groups of regulated persons.

D1 - SELF-EMPLOYED BARRISTERS, CHAMBERS AND BSB AUTHORISED BODIES

- Provision of……………………………………………………………………………..
- Response to……………………………………………………………………………

D2 - BARRISTERS UNDERTAKING PUBLIC ACCESS AND LICENSED ACCESS WORK

- Public ……………………………………………………………………………………
- Licensed…………………………………………………………………………………

D4 - UNREGISTERED BARRISTERS

- There are no subheadings in this section.

D6 - PRICE AND SERVICE TRANSPARENCY RULES FOR SELF-EMPLOYED BARRISTERS, CHAMBERS AND BSB ENTITIES

- <u>Self-employed barristers, chambers and BSB entities</u>

    Publication ……………………………………………………………………………………...

    Provision of ……………………………………………………………………………………

    Bar Standards Board ……………………………………………………………………………

- <u>Self-employed barristers undertaking public access work and BSB entities supplying legal services directly to the public</u>

    Public Access Guidance ………………………………………………………………………..

    Price transparency policy ………………………………………………………………………

    Publication of …………………………………………………………………………………

52

Using the syllabus to build the answer to question A (1)

Once you have finished this book (1)

Activity

> **Technically you should now work through**
>
> — the remainder of Area 1 of the syllabus, i.e. Parts 3 and 4 of the Handbook; and
>
> — <u>**Bar Standards Board Handbook Equality Rules**</u>
>
> Sections 1 & 2;
>
> **in the same way as you have worked through Part 2 of the Handbook .**
>
> **Then**
>
> **You will still need to also work through learning the content of *Areas 2, 3 and 4 of the syllabus*.**
>
> **You may find that a little tedious at this stage!**

In the interests of getting you started on assessment SAQ technique, however, we are going to park your working through the contents of the above box for the time being. It will be picked up in the "Second Half" of this book.

Instead, therefore, we are now going to continue building Question A and the answer to that question, based on the tiny bit of further information we have now got from the Activities on the previous few pages.

Question A

First, here again, for your convenience, is Question A.

Today is Tuesday. You are spending today preparing for a court appearance as Counsel tomorrow. On Thursday and Friday your professional diary states that you are spending those days preparing for a two - day court appearance as Counsel on Monday and Tuesday next week. Your best friend has just telephoned to say that he/she has booked a long weekend for you both in Prague on a flight leaving at 6.30 am this Thursday and returning in the afternoon on Sunday. He/she tells you that they have booked lots of tours and entertainment, so don't expect a minute to yourself! You privately tell your clerk you would like to go as it is your friend's birthday. Next time you are in the reception area of Chambers, where there are solicitors and lay clients waiting to meet with other barristers, your clerk tells you that she has seen other barristers who in similar situations have done their preparation on the plane rather than miss out on a holiday and says that you should do the same. When you later ask her more about that, she says it was a long time ago in different chambers and they are all probably retired by now.

By reference to the applicable Core Duties and other principles of the Handbook, which ethical issues arise from this scenario and how should you resolve them?

Using the syllabus to build the answer to Question A (2)

Let us re-iterate the current content of your recall for the *Conduct Rules*. Here it is again for ease of reference.

The Conduct Rules

YOU AND THE COURT

- *Independence in the interests of justice*
- *Not misleading the court*
- *Not abusing your role as an advocate*

BEHAVING ETHICALLY

- *Honesty, integrity and independence*
- *Referral fees*
- *Undertakings*
- *Discrimination*
- *Foreign work*

YOU AND YOUR CLIENT

1. *Best interests of each client, provision of a competent standard of work and confidentiality*
2. *Not misleading potential clients (see also D6 in area 1 of syllabus, part 2 of the Handbook)*
3. *Personal responsibility*
4. *Accepting Instructions*
5. *Defining terms or basis on which instructions are accepted*
6. *Returning instructions*
7. *Requirement not to discriminate*
8. *The 'cab-rank' rule*

YOU AND YOUR REGULATOR

- *Provision of information to the Bar Standards Board*
- *Duty to report certain matters to the Bar Standards Board*
- *Reporting serious misconduct by others*
- *Access to premises*
- *Co-operation with the Legal Ombudsman*
- *Ceasing to Practice*

YOU AND YOUR PRACTICE

- *Client money*
- *Insurance*
- *Associations with others*
- *Outsourcing*
- *Administration and conduct of self-employed practice*

Using the syllabus to build the answer to Question A (2)

YOU AND THE COURT

You are already aware, from earlier in this book (because I told you so!) that *YOU AND THE COURT* is pertinent to your answer to Question A and that the first element in that section of the Handbook is a *duty to the court to act with independence in the interests of justice.*

Hopefully it is obvious to you that Question A, about appearing in court as Counsel, engages the *YOU AND THE COURT* section of the *Conduct Rules.*

Remember that I also pointed out that the words *'duty to court…interests of justice'* should spark in you the need to also address *CD1*; and the word *'independence'* should spark in you the need to also address *CD4*.

Thus the following detail in the "cloud callout" from *YOU AND THE COURT* needs to be included in an answer to Question A. [The types of "callout" surrounding text are relevant, helping to group like with like, as highlighting them does not show up when printed].

YOU AND THE COURT

> • *Independence CD4 in the interests of justice CD1*

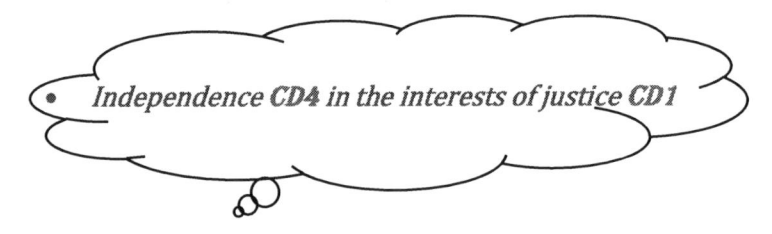

- *Not misleading the court*
- *Not abusing your role as an advocate*

We can therefore now start to build another aide memoir for final revision; that of which CDs should likely be mentioned in addition to each of the *Conduct Rules*. This will build in the Second "Half" of this book. Note that this is not a substitute for being familiar with and manipulating the ethical rules and principles in the way that you should be acquiring them by using this book! Yet some short cuts may be appreciated in the final stages of your revision.

Contents of column (ii) (so far)	
Area of the *Conduct Rules.*	**Associated** *CDS*
YOU AND THE COURT	*1 AND 4* (so far)

You may ask, for instance, why is 'not abusing your role as an advocate' not relevant to Question A? The answer is, that by the time we have built up the whole of the *Conduct Rules* on *YOU AND THE COURT,* you will know what are the only matters and activities which come into the ambit of not "abusing your role as an advocate". The contents of the answer to the scenario in Question A is not one of them.

Hopefully you are now beginning to see why some candidates in the assessments seem to randomly pull, say, 'not abusing your role as an advocate' into a scenario where it is not relevant. Sadly they have committed to memory most if not all of the syllabus; they just have not yet gained the skill of how to analyse a scenario and so how to only apply the relevant parts of the syllabus in their answers.

Using the syllabus to build the answer to Question A (2)

BEHAVING ETHICALLY

You will see from above that the word *'independence'* also appears in this section. It is therefore extremely likely that there will be marks available for referring to this section of the Handbook in answer to your Question A as well.

BEHAVING ETHICALLY

- *Honesty, integrity and* ⟨ *independence CD4* ⟩
- *Referral fees*
- *Undertakings*
- *Discrimination*
- *Foreign work*

Contents of column (ii) (so far)	
Area of the *Conduct Rules.*	**Associated** *CDS*
YOU AND THE COURT	*1 AND 4* (so far)
BEHAVING ETHICALLY	*4* (so far)

(Are you beginning to see how previous candidates may have thought they had given all the detail they needed by mentioning independence only once in answer to Question A? Then are you also beginning to see why they did not gain as many marks as they may have felt they deserved?)

YOU AND YOUR CLIENT

Further, notice how I am highlighting *Personal Responsibility* in the same "callout", in the *YOU AND YOUR CLIENT* section. Again, this sits well alongside independence, doesn't it?

YOU AND YOUR CLIENT

1. *Best interests of each client, provision of a competent standard of work and confidentiality*
2. *Not misleading potential clients (see also D6 in area 1 of syllabus, part 2 of the Handbook)*
3. *Personal responsibility CD4*
4. *Accepting Instructions*
5. *Defining terms or basis on which instructions are accepted*
6. *Returning instructions*
7. *Requirement not to discriminate*
8. *The 'cab-rank' rule*

Contents of column (ii) (so far)	
Area of the *Conduct Rules.*	**Associated** *CDS*
YOU AND THE COURT	1 AND 4 (so far)
BEHAVING ETHICALLY	4 (so far)
YOU AND YOUR CLIENT	4 (so far)

Using the syllabus to build the answer to Question A (2)

Next, the *YOU AND YOUR CLIENT* section. I am highlighting *Best interests of each client*, with its own new "callout" style. This is because not preparing thoroughly means you would not be doing your best for your client.

YOU AND YOUR CLIENT

1. **[Best interests of each client, CD2]** provision of a competent standard of work, and confidentiality
2. *Not misleading potential clients (see also D6 in area 1 of syllabus, part 2 of the Handbook)*
3. *Personal responsibility*
4. *Accepting Instructions*
5. *Defining terms or basis on which instructions are accepted*
6. *Returning instructions*
7. *Requirement not to discriminate*
8. *The 'cab-rank' rule*

| Contents of column (ii) (so far) ||
Area of the *Conduct Rules.*	**Associated** *CDS*
YOU AND THE COURT	1 AND 4 (so far)
BEHAVING ETHICALLY	4 (so far)
YOU AND YOUR CLIENT	2 AND 4 (so far)

Using the syllabus to build the answer to Question A (2)

Then in addition in the *YOU AND YOUR CLIENT* section, I am highlighting *provision of a competent standard of work,* with its own new "callout" style. This is because not preparing thoroughly means that you could you be sure of providing a competent standard of work and service.

YOU AND YOUR CLIENT

1. Best interests of each client, *CD2* *(provision of a competent standard of work, CD7)*

   confidentiality
2. Not misleading potential clients (see also D6 in area 1 of syllabus, part 2 of the Handbook)
3. Personal responsibility
4. Accepting Instructions
5. Defining terms or basis on which instructions are accepted
6. Returning instructions
7. Requirement not to discriminate
8. The 'cab-rank' rule

Contents of column (ii) (so far)	
Area of the *Conduct Rules.*	**Associated** *CDS*
YOU AND THE COURT	*1 AND 4* (so far)
BEHAVING ETHICALLY	*4* (so far)
YOU AND YOUR CLIENT	*2 AND 4 AND 7* (so far)

Using the syllabus to build the answer to Question A (2)

Gathering it all together, our planning for Question A so far looks like this:

YOU AND THE COURT

- *Independence CD4 in the interests of justice CD1*
- Not misleading the court
- Not abusing your role as an advocate

BEHAVING ETHICALLY

- Honesty, integrity and *independence CD4*
- Referral fees
- Undertakings
- Discrimination
- Foreign work

YOU AND YOUR CLIENT

1. Best interests of each client, CD2 *provision of a competent standard of work CD7 and,*

   confidentiality

2. Not misleading potential clients

3. *Personal responsibility CD4*

4. Accepting Instructions
5. Defining terms or basis on which instructions are accepted
6. Returning instructions
7. Requirement not to discriminate
8. The 'cab-rank' rule

Using the syllabus to build the answer to Question A (2)

We are now going to return to the Rubric Planning Template for the answer to Question A to add in this extra information. (There will be more to add later on when we add in the *guidance*).

The table on the next page is the same one that we had created at the end of the section called "Beginning to plan the answer to Question A", with the call outs added, shrunk down to save space and to enable you to pick up from there.

The table on the following page is the continuation of the table in normal size, putting in the detail for *BEHAVING ETHICALLY* AND *YOU AND YOUR CLIENT*.

Using the syllabus to build the answer to Question A (2)

(i) Identify ethical issues. State them generically	(ii) set out the relevant bits of the syllabus **For Question A**
	• *RELEVANT CDS*
	• *Conduct rules (rC)*
	  YOU AND THE COURT
	  BEHAVING ETHICALLY
	  YOU AND YOUR CLIENT
	• *relevant guidance (gC)*
		(iii) apply your knowledge with a reasoned explanation of breach/no breach	(iv) Resolve i.e. advise

Question A			
which ethical issues arise from [this scenario]	By reference to the applicable Core Duties and other principles of the Handbook		and how should you resolve them
Not preparing fully for court	YOU AND THE COURT • *duty to the court to act with independence in the interests of justice*	• Clerk suggests I prepare on the plane. Must make my own decisions and not blindly depend on clerk's advice	• I will make my own decision about whether or not to plan on the plane.
	• CD1	preparing on the plane would be in breach of this duty because I had given myself 2 full days to prepare; it will likely be rushed and not to the best of my abilities. It would not be in the interests of justice if I went to court under prepared.	• I will not prepare on the plane; I will take the 2 days I originally felt I needed to plan for the 2 day court appearance next week.
	• CD4	• Following clerk's suggestion would be breach of this because I must make my own professional decisions independently of anyone else.	• I will tell my friend that my professional duties and ethical principles mean that I cannot go on the trip to Prague this weekend.
	BEHAVING ETHICALLY – broken down in the same way across the columns)	→	→
	YOU AND YOUR CLIENT – broken down in the same way across the columns)	→	→
Second ethical issue, if is one.			

Not preparing fully for court (continued)	BEHAVING ETHICALLY – *independence*	to go in independence section of answer	Is the same resolutiion as in the previous table – "I will make my own decision... etc
	CD4	Ditto	Ditto
	YOU AND YOUR CLIENT – Best interests of each client,	not preparing thoroughly means you would not be doing your best for your client because you would be selling them short.	Prepare thoroughly, not go to Prague
	CD2	ditto	Prepare thoroughly, not go to Prague
	provision of a competent standard of work and service,	neither could you be sure of providing a competent standard of work and service because working on a plane,	The best place to prepare to provide a competent standard of work and service is

Using the syllabus to build the answer to Question A (2)

			sitting next to others, the distractions of snacks and so on on a plane journey is not conducive to full concentration and in turn a competent standard of work and service.	either in Chambers or at home where full quiet and concentration are possible.
		CD7	Ditto	Ditto
		(Personal responsibility)	to go in independence section of answer	Is the same resolution as in the earlier independence issues – "I will make my own decision…. etc
		CD4	Ditto	Ditto
Second ethical issue (if there is one in any given scenario) [73]				

---

[73] Note than there are two elements in our answer for the one issue. It does not matter whether you plan it in this way or whether you plan to answer it as two separate issues, as the same information would appear in your answer either way.

Using the syllabus to build the answer to Question A (2)

So your answer to Question A as it stands at the moment (before further bits of the Handbook are added to it later on to make it a fuller answer) could look something like this. [Again, what we had already created before is in the smaller font, the new elements are in normal size.]

The first ethical issue which arises is potentially not preparing fully for a court appearance. [74]

— There is a rule in the YOU AND THE COURT SECTION OF THE Handbook to the effect that barristers have a duty to the court to (act with independence in the interests of justice.)

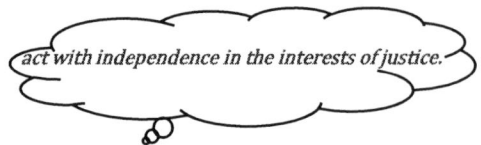

There is also a rule in the BEHAVING ETHICALLY section which begins with rules about honesty, integrity and independence. It is the reference to (independence) that is relevant here. [75]

Further, there is another rule in the YOU AND YOUR CLIENT section about a barrister taking (personal responsibility.) [76]

My clerk suggests I prepare for next week's court appearance on the plane to and from Prague so that I can go there this weekend. I must make my own decisions and not blindly depend on my clerk's advice. It would also be a breach of the rule on independence in the BEHAVING ETHICALLY section of the Handbook and of the rule in YOU AND YOUR CLIENT about a barrister taking personal responsibility if I were not to make my own decisions separately from what my clerk advises about preparing on the plane.

I will resolve this issue by making my own decision about whether or not to plan on the plane.

— ALL BARRISTERS ARE BOUND BY 10 CORE DUTIES (CDS). CD1 IS RELEVANT HERE. IT STATES THAT, "YOU MUST OBSERVE YOUR DUTY TO THE COURT IN THE ADMINISTRATION OF JUSTICE."

Preparing on the plane would be in breach of this duty because I had given myself 2 full days to prepare; it will likely be rushed and not to the best of my abilities if I were to try to do it on the plane. It would not be in the interests of the administration of justice if I went to court under prepared.

I will resolve this issue by not preparing on the plane. I will take the 2 days I originally felt I needed to plan for the 2 day court appearance next week.

— CD4 IS ALSO ENGAGED. IT STATES THAT, "YOU MUST MAINTAIN YOUR INDEPENDENCE". [77]

---

[74] You could equally well have planned to form your answer as 2 issues; one on short preparation time, the other on listening to your clerk's advice. You would come up with the same points in your answer either way.

[75] Notice that no time or effort is wasted on talking about honesty and integrity here. It is not relevant to the scenario.

[76] Notice how all the similar references from column (ii) of the Rubrik Planning Template – those with the same type of "callout"- are grouped together. This means that where, in columns (ii) and (iv) the same content is relevant, you will only need to set it out once I your written answer.

[77] No need to repeat CD4, even though it appears in your plan more than once, as it does not change whether it flashes to your mind via *YOU AND THE COURT* or via *BEHAVING ETHICALLY* or via YOU AND YOUR CLIENT

Using the syllabus to build the answer to Question A (2)

Following my clerk's suggestion would be breach of CD4 because I must make my own professional decisions independently of anyone else.

I will further resolve this issue by telling my friend that my professional duties and ethical principles mean that I cannot go on the trip to Prague this weekend. I will take Thursday and Friday this week to plan fully that I originally deemed I need. [78]

The YOU AND YOUR CLIENT section of the Conduct rules in the Handbook begins with a rule that a barrister has a duty to act in the best interests of each client.

CORE DUTY 2 SIMILARLY STATES THAT, "YOU MUST ACT IN THE BEST INTERESTS OF EACH CLIENT."

Not preparing thoroughly, preparing only on the plane, would be a breach of that Conduct Rule and that Core Duty because I would not be doing my best for my client as I would be selling them short.

I should take the full 2 days to plan in a professional working environment, as I had originally planned to do.

There is a rule in the YOU AND YOUR CLIENT section of the Conduct rules in the Handbook requiring the provision of a competent standard of work to each client.

CORE DUTY 7 IS ALSO ENGAGED. THIS STATES THAT, "YOU MUST MUST PROVIDE A COMPETENT STANDARD OF WORK AND SERVICE [79] TO EACH CLIENT."

I could not be sure of providing a competent standard of work and service [80] to my clients because working on a plane, sitting next to others, the distractions of snacks and so on on a plane journey is not conducive to full concentration and in turn not conducive to a competent standard of work and service. I would therefore be in breach of this rule and this CD were I to try to cut corners and do that, so that I could go on the long weekend to Prague.

The best place to prepare to provide a competent standard of work and service is either in Chambers or at home where full quiet and concentration are possible.

---

[78] Moved to be my final conclusion during planning.
[79] Notice how CD7 adds in the word "service"
[80] Notice how CD7 adds in the word "service"

I will further resolve this issue by telling my friend that my professional duties and ethical principles mean that I cannot go on the trip to Prague this weekend. I will take Thursday and Friday this week to plan fully that I originally deemed I need.

The second ethical issue which arises is......

Using the syllabus to build the answer to Question A (2)

In actual fact, now is the time to contribute further to your incremental learning of the contents of the syllabus here using only those further elements of the rules that are relevant to answering Question A.[81]

Here is where we were up to in our planning. This time those areas of the syllabus that we have identified as not relevant to Question A have been deleted.

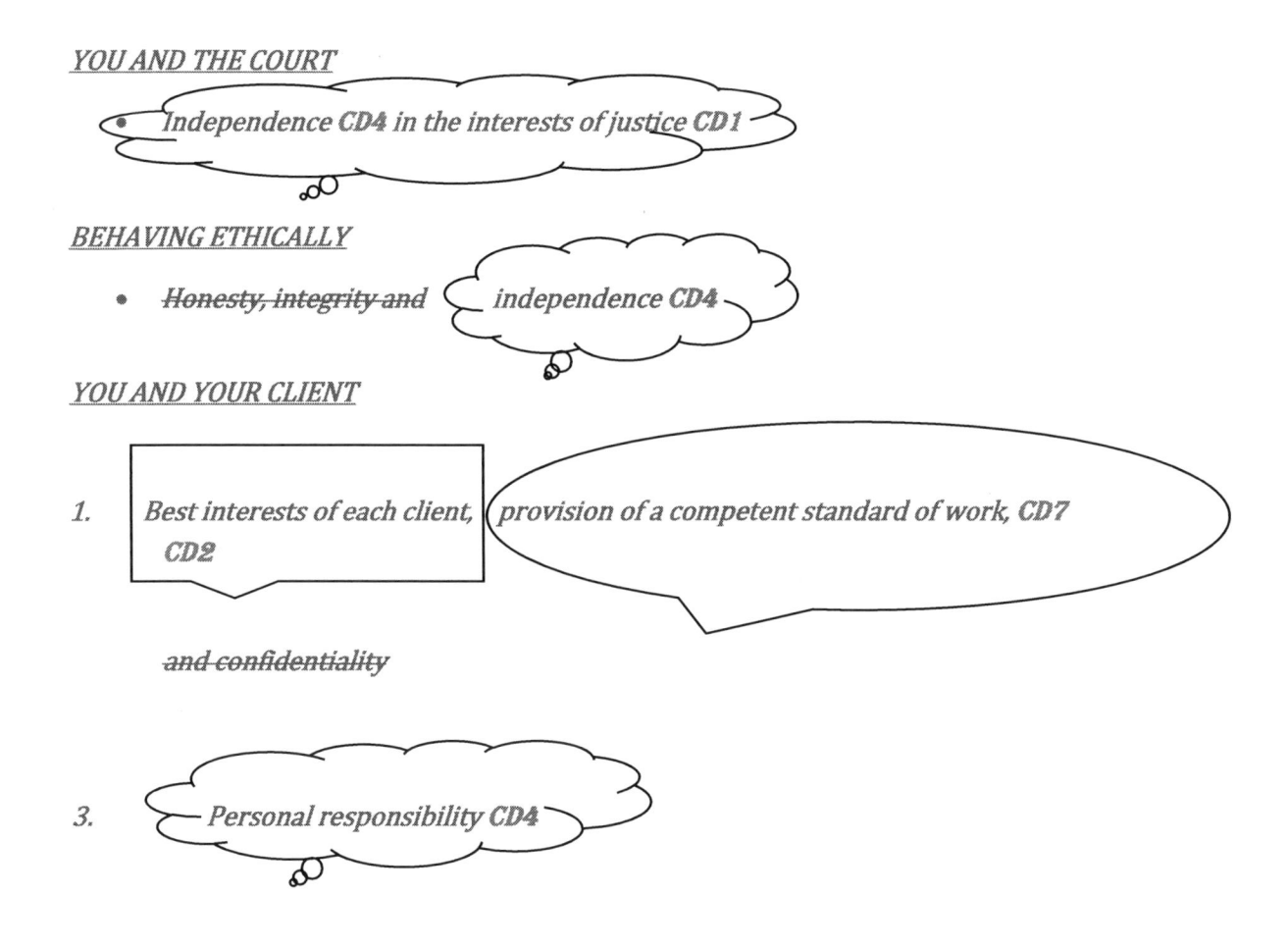

YOU AND THE COURT

- *Independence CD4 in the interests of justice CD1*

BEHAVING ETHICALLY

- ~~*Honesty, integrity and*~~ *independence CD4*

YOU AND YOUR CLIENT

1. *Best interests of each client, CD2, provision of a competent standard of work, CD7*

   ~~*and confidentiality*~~

3. *Personal responsibility CD4*

---

[81] The whole of *YOU AND THE COURT*, will be broken down for you in the Second "Half" of this book, with the opportunity for you to break down *BEHAVING ETHICALLY* and *YOU AND YOUR CLIENT* in the same way.

Using the syllabus to build the answer to Question A (2)

Now we will add in the next increments relevant to Question A to this plan of the contents of column (ii) of the Rubrik Planning Template,

The Conduct Rules

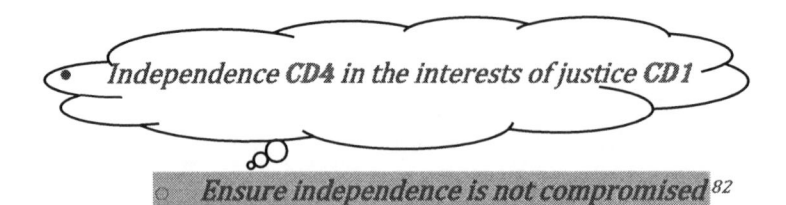

<u>YOU AND THE COURT</u>

- *Independence CD4 in the interests of justice CD1*
  - Ensure independence is not compromised [82]

<u>BEHAVING ETHICALLY</u>

- *independence CD4*
  - Do not undermine your independence [83]

<u>YOU AND YOUR CLIENT</u>

2. Best interests of each client, CD2 | provision of a competent standard of work and service, CD7
   - There is no further breakdown relative to Question A

3. *Personal responsibility CD4*
   - Use your own professional judgment and be able to justify your decisions and actions, notwithstanding the views of other. [84]

---

[82] This is the relevant sub-rule extracted from the *'independence'* "heading" – first row of *rc3* in the BSB Handbook - in *YOU AND THE COURT*. [It is actually *rC 3.5* although you do not need to know the number in your assessment].

[83] This is the relevant rule extracted from the word *'independence'* in the red heading *BEHAVING ETHICALLY* in the BSB Handbook. [It is actually *rC 8* although you do not need to know the number in your assessment].

[84] This is the relevant rule extracted from the word *'Personal responsibility'* in the red heading *YOU AND YOUR CLIENT* in the BSB Handbook. [It is actually *rC 20* although you do not need to know the number in your assessment].

i.e.

YOU AND THE COURT

- *Independence in the interests of justice*
  - *Ensure independence is not compromised*

BEHAVING ETHICALLY

- *independence*
  - *Do not undermine your independence*

YOU AND YOUR CLIENT

- *Best interests of each client, provision of a competent standard of work*
- *Personal responsibility*
  - *Use your own professional judgment and be able to justify your decisions and actions, notwithstanding the views of others.*

Adding this into your Rubric Planning Template produces the table which starts on the next page. What we have produced until now is reproduced in small font. What is new is in normal size font.

Using the syllabus to build the answer to Question A (2)

(i) Identify ethical issues. State them generically	ii) set out the relevant bits of the syllabus
	For Question A
	• *RELEVANT CDS*
	• Conduct rules (rC)
	  YOU AND THE COURT
	  BEHAVING ETHICALLY
	  YOU AND YOUR CLIENT
	• *relevant guidance (gC)*
		(iii) apply your knowledge with a reasoned explanation of breach/no breach	(iv) Resolve i.e. advise

Question A			
which ethical issues arise from [this scenario]	By reference to the applicable Core Duties and other principles of the Handbook		and how should you resolve them
Not preparing fully for court	YOU AND THE COURT • *(duty to the court to act with independence in the interests of justice)* • **Ensure independence is not compromised** • CD1	• Clerk suggests I prepare on the plane. Must make my own decisions and not blindly depend on clerk's advice *It would be compromised if I did not make my own decision on this* preparing on the plane would be in breach of this duty because I had given myself 2 full days to prepare; it will likely be rushed and not to the best of my	• I will make my own decision about whether or not to plan on the plane. I will ensure that my independence is not compromised. I will know that I have done the right thing. • I will not prepare on the plane, I will take the 2 days I originally felt I needed to plan or

Using the syllabus to build the answer to Question A (2)

	• CD4	abilities. It would not be in the interests of justice if I went to court under prepared. • Following clerk's suggestion would be breach of this because I must make my own professional decisions independently of anyone else.	the 2 day court appearance next week. • I will tell my friend that my professional duties and ethical principles mean that I cannot go on the trip to Prague this weekend.
Not preparing fully for court (continued)	BEHAVING ETHICALLY – *Independence* (thought cloud)	To go in independence section of answer	Is the same resolution as in the previous table – "I will make my own decision....etc.
	• **Do not undermine your independence**	Following the suggestion of my clerk to work on the plane would be a breach of this rule because I would not be acting independently as I know the rules require me to	Ditto
	CD4	Ditto	Ditto

74

Using the syllabus to build the answer to Question A (2)

	YOU AND YOUR CLIENT		
	Best interests of each client,	not preparing thoroughly means you would not be doing your best for your client because you would be selling them short.	Prepare thoroughly, not go to Prague
	CD2	ditto	Prepare thoroughly, not go to Prague
	provision of a competent standard of work and service,	neither could you be sure of providing a competent standard of work and service because working on a plane, sitting next to others, the distractions of snacks and so on on a plane journey is not conducive to full concentration and in turn a competent standard of work and service.	The best place to prepare to provide a competent standard of work and service is either in Chambers or at home where full quiet and concentration are possible.
	CD7	Ditto	Ditto

Using the syllabus to build the answer to Question A (2)

	(Personal responsibility)	to go in independence section of answer	Is the same resolutiion as in the earlier independence issues — "I will make my own decision....etc
	Use your own professional judgment and be able to justify your decisions and actions, notwithstanding the views of others.	*If I were to work on the plane it would be very difficult to justify that decision. It would also be a breach if I took on board the views of the clerk to do so, since I know that the rules and my professional responsibilities go against this.*	Ditto
	CD4	Ditto	Ditto
Second ethical issue (if there is one in any given scenario) [85]			

---

[85] Note than there are two elements in our answer for the one issue. It does not matter whether you plan it in this way or whether you plan to answer it as two separate issues, as the same information would appear in your answer either way.

Using the syllabus to build the answer to Question A (2)

So your answer to Question A as it stands at the moment (before further bits of the Handbook are added to it later on to make it a fuller answer) could look something like this. [Again, what we had already created before is in the smaller font, the new elements are in normal size.]

The first ethical issue which arises is potentially not preparing fully for a court appearance.

— There is a rule in the YOU AND THE COURT SECTION OF THE Handbook to the effect that barristers have a duty to the court to *act with independence in the interests of justice.* The rule goes on to say that they must ensure that their **independence is not compromised**.

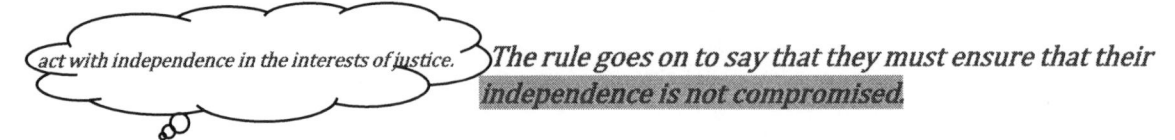

There is also a rule in the BEHAVING ETHICALLY section which begins with rules about honesty, integrity and independence. It is the reference to *independence* that is relevant here. **Do not undermine your independence**.

Further, there is another rule in the YOU AND YOUR CLIENT section about a barrister taking *personal responsibility*.

Use your own professional judgment and be able to justify your decisions and actions notwithstanding the views of others.

My clerk suggests I prepare for next week's court appearance on the plane to and from Prague so that I can go there this weekend. I must make my own decisions and not blindly depend on my clerk's advice.

My independence would be compromised if I did not make my own decision on this.

Following the suggestion of my clerk to work on the plane would be a breach of the rule not to undermine my independence because I would not be acting independently, as I know the rules require me to act independently.

It would also be a breach of the rule on independence in the BEHAVING ETHICALLY section of the Handbook and of the rule in YOU AND YOUR CLIENT about a barrister taking personal responsibility if I were not to make my own decisions separately from what my clerk advises about preparing on the plane.

If I were to work on the plane it would be very difficult to justify that decision. It would also be a breach if I took on board the views of the clerk to do so, since I know that the rules and my professional responsibilities go against this.

I will resolve this issue by making my own decision about whether or not to plan on the plane.

I will ensure that my independence is not compromised. I will know that I have done the right thing. Just to be sure, if anyone was in chambers when the clerk suggested this should hear me say that I will make my own decision; or if they did not, they will see that I did not go to Prague.

— ALL BARRISTERS ARE BOUND BY 10 CORE DUTIES (CDS). CD1 IS RELEVANT HERE. IT STATES THAT, "YOU MUST OBSERVE YOUR DUTY TO THE COURT IN THE ADMINISTRATION OF JUSTICE."

Preparing on the plane would be in breach of this duty because I had given myself 2 full days to prepare; it will likely be rushed and not to the best of my abilities if I were to try to do it on the plane. It would not be in the interests of the administration of justice if I went to court under prepared.

I will resolve this issue by not preparing on the plane. I will take the 2 days I originally felt I needed to plan for the 2 day court appearance next week.

CD4 IS ALSO ENGAGED. IT STATES THAT, "YOU MUST MAINTAIN YOUR INDEPENDENCE".

Following my clerk's suggestion would be breach of CD4 because I must make my own professional decisions independently of anyone else.

The YOU AND YOUR CLIENT section of the Conduct rules in the Handbook begins with a rule that a barrister has a duty to act in the best interests of each client. **CORE DUTY 2 SIMILARLY STATES THAT, "YOU MUST ACT IN THE BEST INTERESTS OF EACH CLIENT."**

Not preparing thoroughly, preparing only on the plane, would be a breach of that Conduct Rule and that Core Duty because I would not be doing my best for my client as I would be selling them short.

I should take the full 2 days to plan in a professional working environment, as I had originally planned to do.

There is a rule in the YOU AND YOUR CLIENT section of the Conduct rules in the Handbook requiring the provision of a competent standard of work to each client. **CORE DUTY 7 IS ALSO ENGAGED. THIS STATES THAT, "YOU MUST MUST PROVIDE A COMPETENT STANDARD OF WORK AND SERVICE TO EACH CLIENT."**

I could not be sure of providing a competent standard of work and service to my clients because working on a plane, sitting next to others, the distractions of snacks and so on on a plane journey is not conducive to full concentration and in turn not conducive to a competent standard of work and service. I would therefore be in breach of this rule and this CD were I to try to cut corners and do that, so that I could go on the long weekend to Prague.

The best place to prepare to provide a competent standard of work is either in Chambers or at home where full quiet and concentration are possible.

I will further resolve this issue by telling my friend that my professional duties and ethical principles mean that I cannot go on the trip to Prague this weekend. I will take Thursday and Friday this week to plan fully that I originally deemed I need.[86]

Here is how our answer to Question A is looking so far. Subheadings have been added in to help the marker notice that I am following the assessment rubric.

Ethical Issue

The ethical issue which arises is potentially not preparing fully for a court appearance.

Describe relevant parts of the ethics syllabus

There is a rule in the YOU AND THE COURT SECTION OF THE Handbook to the effect that barristers have a duty to the court to act with independence in the interests of justice. The rule goes on to say that they must ensure that their independence is not compromised.

---

[86] Notice how each section of the answer definitely contains columns (i) (ii) (iii) and (iv) of the Rubric Planning Template. Thus it definitely follows the requirements of the assessment rubric. The paragraph beginning *CD4 IS ALSO ENGAGED* is the only one that does not show the column (iv) advice/resolution. Remember that it is because it felt better to use it as the final concluding paragraph to the question, insofar as our answer currently goes.

Using the syllabus to build the answer to Question A (2)

There is also a rule in the BEHAVING ETHICALLY section which begins with rules about honesty, integrity and independence. It is the reference to independence that is relevant here. Do not undermine your independence.

Further, there is another rule in the YOU AND YOUR CLIENT section about a barrister taking personal responsibility. Use your own professional judgment and be able to justify your decisions and actions notwithstanding the views of others.

<u>Reasoned explanation, applying the above knowledge of ethics regarding whether or not there has been a breach.</u>

My clerk suggests I prepare for next week's court appearance on the plane to and from Prague so that I can go there this weekend. I must make my own decisions and not blindly depend on my clerk's advice.

My independence would be compromised if I did not make my own decision on this.

Following the suggestion of my clerk to work on the plane would be a breach of the rule not to undermine my independence because I would not be acting independently, as I know the rules require me to act independently.

It would also be a breach of the rule on independence in the BEHAVING ETHICALLY section of the Handbook and of the rule in YOU AND YOUR CLIENT about a barrister taking personal responsibility if I were not to make my own decisions separately from what my clerk advises about preparing on the plane.

If I were to work on the plane it would be very difficult to justify that decision. It would also be a breach if I took on board the views of the clerk to do so, since I know that the rules and my professional responsibilites go against this.

<u>How I should resolve this</u>

I will resolve this issue by making my own decision about whether or not to plan on the plane.

I will ensure that my independence is not compromised. I will know that I have done the right thing. Just to be sure, if anyone was in chambers when the clerk suggested this should hear me say that I will make my own decision; or if they dd not, they will see that I did not go to Prague.

<u>Describe relevant parts of the ethics syllabus</u>

All barristers are bound by 10 Core Duties (CDs). CD1 is relevant here. It states that, "you must observe your duty to the court in the administration of justice."

<u>Reasoned explanation, applying the above knowledge of ethics regarding whether or not there has been a breach.</u>

Preparing on the plane would be in breach of this duty because I had given myself 2 full days to prepare; it will likely be rushed and not to the best of my abilities if I were to try to do it on the plane. It would not be in the interests of the administration of justice if I went to court under prepared.

Using the syllabus to build the answer to Question A (2)

How I should resolve this

I will resolve this issue by not preparing on the plane. I will take the 2 days I originally felt I needed to plan for the 2 day court appearance next week.

— Describe relevant parts of the ethics syllabus

CD4 is also engaged. It states that, "you must maintain your independence".

Reasoned explanation, applying the above knowledge of ethics regarding whether or not there has been a breach.

Following my clerk's suggestion would be breach of CD4 because I must make my own professional decisions independently of anyone else.

— Describe relevant parts of the ethics syllabus

The YOU AND YOUR CLIENT section of the Conduct rules in the Handbook begins with a rule that a barrister has a duty to act in the best interests of each client. Core Duty 2 similarly states that, "You must act in the best interests of each client."

Reasoned explanation, applying the above knowledge of ethics regarding whether or not there has been a breach.

Not preparing thoroughly, preparing only on the plane, would be a breach of that Conduct Rule and that Core Duty because I would not be doing my best for my client as I would be selling them short.

How I should resolve this

I should take the full 2 days to plan in a professional working environment, as I had originally planned to do.

— Describe relevant parts of the ethics syllabus

There is a rule in the YOU AND YOUR CLIENT section of the Conduct rules in the Handbook requiring the provision of a competent standard of work to each client.

Core duty 7 is also engaged. This states that, "You must must provide a competent standard of work and service [87] to each client."

Reasoned explanation, applying the above knowledge of ethics regarding whether or not there has been a breach.

I could not be sure of providing a competent standard of work and service to my clients because working on a plane, sitting next to others, the distractions of snacks and so on on a plane journey is not conducive to full concentration and in turn not conducive to a competent standard of work and service. I would therefore be in breach of this rule and this CD were I to try to cut corners and do that, so that I could go on the long weekend to Prague.

---

[87] Notice that CD7 includes the word 'service' inn addition

Using the syllabus to build the answer to Question A (2)

How I should resolve this

The best place to prepare to provide a competent standard of work is either in Chambers or at home where full quiet and concentration are possible.

I will further resolve this issue by telling my friend that my professional duties and ethical principles mean that I cannot go on the trip to Prague this weekend. I will take Thursday and Friday this week to plan fully that I originally deemed I need.

BUT WE HAVEN'T FINISHED ANSWERING QUESTION A YET.

Remember that the question asks for

"reference to the applicable Core Duties AND OTHER PRINCIPLES OF THE HANDBOOK".

At this point, we have reached an answer which deals with these relevant principles of the Handbook:

- *Conduct Rules* from the relevant sections of the Handbook, those being
  - *YOU AND THE COURT,*
  - *BEHAVING ETHICALLY* and
  - *YOU AND YOUR CLIENT* and
- the applicable *CORE DUTIES*

That means we have still to add in any relevant *guidance* to those conduct rule principles. We WILL add these in later.

No other "principles of the Handbook" are intended to be engaged by this Question A.

You would be right to question at this point the length that the answer has already reached.

And we still have to add in the *guidance.*

And we have only 2.5 hours to read, plan and write 6 answers.[88]

---

[88] We will also address how to reduce the time you spend planning and the size of your answer later, trimming it down to only those kind of points which attracted marks in 2017.

Timing

This seems like a good time to talk some more about good assessment techniques.

I am sure that in this section we will not be dealing with anything new to you. Sadly though, some scripts do show evidence of mushed assessment brain taking over from logical and strict assessment brain.

The assessment is 2 hours and 30 minutes long [150 minutes].

There are 6 questions to answer.

That means 25 minutes per question; to read it, plan it, write it out.

That means approximately

— 25 mins per 10 marks
— 12 mins for 5 marks
— 10 minutes for 4 marks
— 6 mins for 2 or 3 marks.

So

— move to question 2 at 2.25pm
— move to question 3 at 2.50pm
— move to question 4 at 3.15pm
— move to question 5 at 3.40pm
— move to question 6 at 4.05pm.

Should you personally, for any reason, be a candidate who is allowed more than 2.5 hours for the assessment, you would be wise to plan the time to move on to the next question before you get to the assessment room.

MAKE YOURSELF STOP AFTER THE NUMBER OF MINUTES ALLOTTED FOR THE TOTAL NUMBER OF MARKS PER QUESTION OR SUB QUESTION.

Honestly, there really is no time to spend longer than the 25 minutes on each question. Remember the adage that in a 10 mark question, it is the first few marks that are relatively easy to get onto your assessment script. On that basis you would therefore be unwise to spend more than the allotted time on each question. Why eat into the time for another question by trying to get 8, 9 or 10 out of 10 on one question, when you are doing that at the expense of the easier marks to get when beginning to answer the next question? It may be better to move on, hopefully gaining at least 7/10 on 6 questions, rather than, say, 9/10, 7/10, 5/10, 3/10, 1/10, 0/10 by allowing time to slip.

The former technique would give you 42/60; the latter 25/60.

You normally have to gain 36 out of 60 or equivalent to pass; that's 6 marks out of 10 per question.

Please do practise, during your revision, timings that work for you – how long to plan, how long to write out your answer - and incorporate that into your timings if you can.

Please also bear in mind as you work through this book that your thought processes in the assessment need to achieve all that is in this book 6 times for a maximum of 25 minutes each question.

Timing

There follow some hints and suggestions on how to do that.

Here again for ease of reference is Question A.

Question A

Today is Tuesday. You are spending today preparing for a court appearance as Counsel tomorrow. On Thursday and Friday your professional diary states that you are spending those days preparing for a two - day court appearance as Counsel on Monday and Tuesday next week. Your best friend has just telephoned to say that he/she has booked a long weekend for you both in Prague on a flight leaving at 6.30 am this Thursday and returning in the afternoon on Sunday. He/she tells you that they have booked lots of tours and entertainment, so don't expect a minute to yourself! You privately tell your clerk you would like to go as it is your friend's birthday. Next time you are in the reception area of Chambers, where there are solicitors and lay clients waiting to meet with other barristers, your clerk tells you that she has seen other barristers who in similar situations have done their preparation on the plane rather than miss out on a holiday and says that you should do the same. When you later ask her more about that, she says it was a long time ago in different chambers and they are all probably retired by now.

By reference to the applicable Core Duties and other principles of the Handbook, which ethical issues arise from this scenario and how should you resolve them?

Hint one

Develop your own shorthand, rather than longhand, when creating your Rubric Planning Template

Here again for ease of reference is the content of your column (ii) so far, written in note form.

YOU AND THE COURT

- *Duty to court = Independence CD4 in the interests of justice CD1*
  - *Ensure not comp*

BEHAVING ETHICALLY

- *Independence*
  - *Not undermine*

YOU AND YOUR CLIENT

- *Best interests of each client, CD2, provision of a competent standard of work AND SERVICE to each client CD7*
- *Personal responsibility*
  - *Own pj; justify d and a. nwt others*

On the next page is one version of a possible Rubric Planning Template you could produce in the assessment, so far for Question A, including the *CORE DUTIES* and the *Conduct Rules.*

(Remember that the *guidance* to the *Conduct Rules* will be added in later).

This next one may not make any sense to you whatsoever – the hieroglyphs may well only mean something only to the person who created the template. It is just another suggested way of achieving the same content in your answer to Question A that we just completed; this time, the ethical issues have been separated into 2 different ones.

There is no one correct way to structure your answer; whether you identified the issue as 'not preparing fully for court' or as 2 issues, 'doing what your clerk suggests' and 'taking less time to plan' will still provide the same answer on your Rubrik Planning Table.

The point is, that fully revised to recall with speed the syllabus and then identify the relevant parts of it, it is hoped you can by then achieve your Rubric Planning Template in fewer than 12 minutes of the 25 minutes you have to allot per question.

Note the lack of lines in the template apart from the one dividing the 2 issues. Anything to save time! DO spend a little time perusing and working through the table on the next two pages. Perhaps you could adapt your planning style into one of such brevity.

Note the extra CD column for sake of clarity.

The fonts/colour coding are retained simply for teaching purposes.

(i)	(ii) (a)	(ii) (b)	(iii)	(iv)
ethl iss	CDS → +Handbook rules		*Explain/apply*	*Advise, resolve*
Do as clerk suggests?	1. Indep in interests of justice; not comp	4 1	*Clerk says plane* *Breach if do as C says ≠ indep. List to C on this wd=comp*	*Make own dec*
	2. Indep, not undermine		*To blindly take adv=undermine idep*	"
	3. Pers resp, Own pj; justify d and a. nwt others	↓	*Breach if list as nwt others. C in this categ. Hard to justify. Breach my own fault*	"
		4. CD1	*CD1. not in interests of just if rush prep*	*Don't rush prep*
		5. CD4	*CD4. prep on plane as c said others do as c said to =breach if not my own decision*	*Make own dec*

Take less time to plan?			*I need 2 days to plan*	
	1) Best int of each cl	2	*No. Breach if squash into plane journey. Distractions*	Don't squash into plane journey
	2) Comp work	7 AND SERV	*Squash in plane journey raises chances of not competent so would be breach*	Take the 2 days I originally diarised for
		3) CD2	*not in cl best int unless I work quietly at home/chambers*	Work in chamber/ at home as orig. Don't go Prague.
		4) CD7	*ditto*	ditto

Regarding the extra CD column for sake of clarity, we now have what could be referred to as column *(ii) (a)* for *The Conduct Rules* and column *(II) (B)* for the CORE DUTIES.

Give yourself a large space to prepare your Rubric Planning Template, perhaps on the back page of each question in the question booklet, or a page in your answer booklet which you later cross out.

Remember to do all 4 columns for each *CD* and each 'other provision of the Handbook'.

REMEMBER THAT IT WAS THE APPLICATION IN COLUMN (III) AND THE RESOLUTION/ADVICE IN COLUMN (IV) THAT STUDENTS SEEMED TO MISS OUT THE MOST IN THE 2017 ASSESSMENTS.

I repeat - remember to do column (iii) for the CDs as well – it could easily be forgotten otherwise;

I repeat - remember to do column (iv) for the CDs as well – it could easily be forgotten otherwise.

It really doesn't matter whether your style develops such that

— you go down through each column in your answer, as we did in the earlier longer version of it; or
— you work along each row of the template to formulate your answer as we will do in the next version of the answer.

It really doesn't matter whether your style develops such that

— it seems impossible to fill in all 4 columns when planning at speed. Just try. It is awareness of the need to address columns (iii) and (iv) that I am trying to get over as the message.

It really doesn't matter whether your style develops such that

— you fill in the template in an order that isn't that of the template. e.g. the latest template above started out as on the next page. (Lines have been left in just to make the structure as clear as possible for explanation purposes).

//
(i)	(ii) (a)	(ii) (b)	(iii)	(iv)
ethl iss	*CDS* +Handbook *rules*	▶	*Explain/apply*	*Advise, resolve*
Do as clerk suggests?			*Clerk says plane*	
Take less time to plan?			*I need 2 days to plan*	

Hint Two

Include in your written Rubric Planning Template only the prompts you need.

To save more time, you may not need to put the contents of columns (iii) and (iv) into your Rubric Planning Template by the time it comes to the assessment. You may have devised a method for simply remembering to include them in your answer! For instance

Your Rubric Planning Template in the assessment could instead look like this:

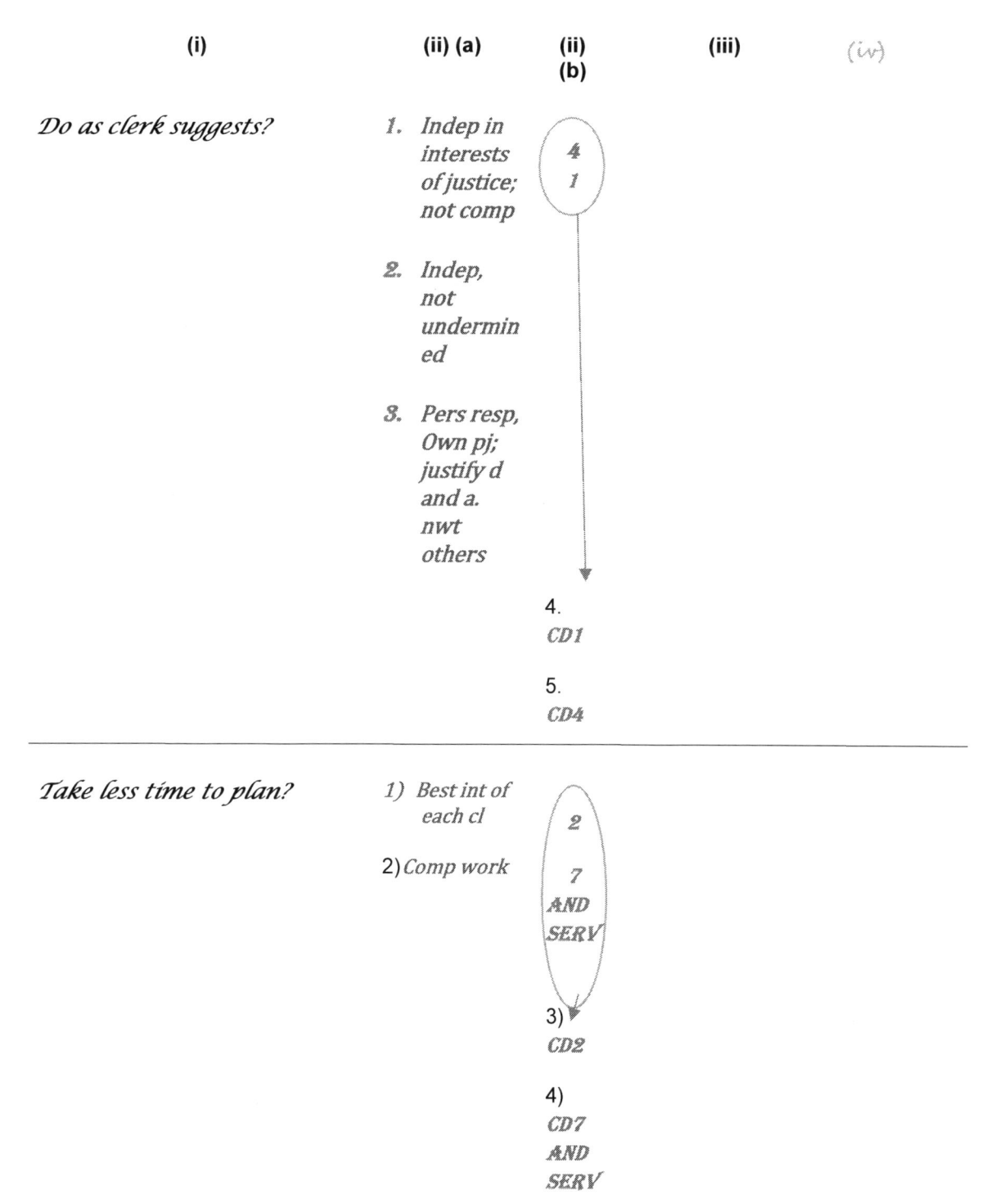

(i)	(ii) (a)	(ii) (b)	(iii)	(iv)

Do as clerk suggests?

1. Indep in interests of justice; not comp   (4 / 1)
2. Indep, not undermined
3. Pers resp, Own pj; justify d and a. nwt others

   ↓

4. CD1
5. CD4

Take less time to plan?

1) Best int of each cl   (2)
2) Comp work   (7 AND SERV)

   3) ↓ CD2
   4) CD7 AND SERV

92

Hint Three

Finish your planning and thinking before you start to write your answer.

Remember that you have around 12 minutes before you need to finish your planning.

It is essential to complete all the content needed your planning for columns (ii) (a)*BSB Handbook rules* **and (ii) (b)** *CORE DUTIES* [and later column (ii) (c) *guidance (gC)]* on those *rules.*

The most awful answers in final assessments are where students have been thinking as they write. This very often leads them to meander off piste in a very disorderly and disastrous fashion. And then time slips, so that later answers suffer from this.

When writing out your answer, use your Rubric Planning Template and keep referring to it so that you do not inadvertently miss out anything from your answer. Perhaps cross out parts of your Rubric Planning Template once you have put them into your answer; perhaps train yourself to put a tick in your empty columns (iii) and (iv) as you address them in your answer

You have around 12 minutes to write out your answer, which will only require you to put your Rubric Planning Template into words. No thinking necessary, just writing!

Hint Four

Include only the relevant elements of a *rule* in your answer.

Be sure that you will not be wasting time by including all the elements on one rule, where only one of the elements to the rule is actually pertinent to the answer.

Here is an extreme example of that, to get the message across.

Suppose that an answer requires you to consider client confidentially. As this is about your client, you are going to include anything on confidentiality from *YOU AND YOUR CLIENT.* You recall that it included in the heading in that section of the *conduct rules* which reads *"Best interests of each client, provision of a competent standard of work and confidentiality".*

The first rule in this section is divided into 5 sub-rules. I recommend that you do not include the wording of all 5 sub-rules (unless the scenario under consideration definitely requires it); include only those that relate to confidentiality.

Otherwise you will have wasted time writing out about a dozen rows of the *rule,* where far fewer than that are necessary and it is only the necessary sub-rule that attracts marks on the mark scheme.

There are plenty more references to confidentiality on the syllabus which you should include for an outstanding answer, so use your time referring to those from across all four columns of your Rubric Planning Template.

Timing

Hint Five

Drop the names of the sections of the Handbook from your answer

There were no marks in the 2017 assessments for setting out the headings of e.g.

~~*YOU AND THE COURT,*~~

~~*BEHAVING ETHICALLY*~~ and

~~*YOU AND YOUR CLIENT.*~~

So although you will use them initially when analysing the scenario, to identify which of the areas are correct to use in your answer, you need not refer to these headings in your answer.

Therefore, we are dropping them from inclusion in our actual answer from now on.

Hint Six

Reduce the previous wordy answer we had,

yet retain those elements which attract the marks.

Answer to Question A

(i) [89]

First Issue - Doing as my clerk suggests

Space – leave at least a page to fill in columns (ii)(a), (ii)(b) [and later (ii)(c)], (iii) and (iv).

(i) [90]

Second Issue - Taking less time to plan for next week's court hearing

Space – leave at least a page to fill in columns (ii)(a), (ii)(b) [and later (ii)(c)], (iii) and (iv)].

---

[89] This (i) refers to column (i) of the Rubric Planning Template
[90] This (i) refers to column (i) of the Rubric Planning Template

Timing

Your answer book (or your plan) could look like this at this point:-

(i) *First Issue - Doing as my clerk suggests*
(ii) [91]
    a) [92] Handbook [93]
        1.[94]

        (iii) [95] *Application*

        (iv) [96] *Resolution*

        2. Handbook

        (iii) *Application*

        (iv) *Resolution*

        3. Handbook

        (iii) *Application*

        (iv) *Resolution*

---

[91] This (ii) refers to column (ii) of the Rubric Planning Template
[92] This (a) refers to column (ii) (a) of the Rubric Planning Template
[93] *Please remember that we will be adding in what will be column (ii) (c), guidance, later.*
[94] This refers to number 1, the first item in your column (ii) (a) of your Rubric Planning Template
[95] This (iii) refers to the contents of column (iii) of the Rubric Planning Template for the first item. Remember we are reading ACROSS the ROWS this time.
[96] This (iv) refers to column (iv) of your Rubric Planning Template for the first item.

Timing

(ii) (b) [97] *CORE DUTIES* [98]

    4.   *CD1*

        (iii)   *Application*

        (iv)   *Resolution*

    5.   *CD4*

        (iii)   *Application*

        (iv)   *Resolution*

---

[97] This (ii) (b) refers to column (ii) (b) of the Rubric Planning Template
[98] This time we have separated out the CDs from the rules which prompted our use of them. It may be that a mark scheme has marks available for application and resolution of rules and CDs separately; this technique may therefore add to your mark tally.

(i)   Second Issue – Taking less time to plan for next week's court hearing

Activity

> You may wish to use the Rubric Planning Template for the Second Issue in Question A to plan the outline of your answer to that issue with spaces for your answer as we have just done for the First Issue.
>
> Please use the two following blank pages for this.

Intentionally Blank

Intentionally Blank

Timing

Once you have filled in the spaces, your answer to the First Issue (before *guidance*) could look like this.

(i) *First Issue - Doing as my clerk suggests*

(ii)   a)   Handbook rules
1. A barrister must act with independence in the interests of justice. That independence should not be compromised.

(iii) *Application*
It would be a breach of these rules if I blindly do as C says and take my planning to do on the plane as I would not be acting independently.

(iv) *Resolution*
I must make my own independent decision.

(ii) Handbook rules
2. I must not allow my independence to be undermined.

(iii) *Application*
Taking the advice from my clerk to do my planning on the plane would undermine my independence and would be a breach of this rule.

(iv) *Resolution*
I must make my own independent decision.

(ii) Handbook rules
3. A barrister
is personally responsible;
must use their own professional judgment; and
be able to justify their decisions and actions, notwithstanding the views of others.

(iii) *Application*
It would be a breach of this rule to take the clerk's advice without using my own professional judgment. I must decide what I decide notwithstanding her advice. Paring down 2 days' preparation to a couple of hours on a busy plane on my clerk's advice alone would mean that my client and the court were not best served by such a shortcut. Planning on a busy plane would be hard to justify.

(iv) *Resolution*
I must make my own independent decision.

Timing

(II) (B) CORE DUTIES

    4. CD1 STATES THAT "YOU MUST OBSERVE YOUR DUTY TO THE COURT IN THE ADMINISTRATION OF JUSTICE."

(iii)   *Application*
It would be a breach of this CD as I would not be observing my duty to the court if I did not prepare as fully as I should.

(iv)   *Resolution*
I must prepare as fully and professionally as I can.

    5. CD4 STATES THAT "YOU MUST MAINTAIN YOUR INDEPENDENCE".

(iii)   *Application*
Following my clerk's suggestion would be breach of CD4 because I must make my own professional decisions independently of anyone else.

(iv)   *Resolution*
I must make my own independent decision

Please remember that we will be adding in what will be column (II) (c), guidance, later.

Activity

You may wish to use your Rubric Planning Template for the Second Issue in Question A to practise your final assessment answer so far in relation to the Second Issue of Question A.

Please use the following three blank pages for this.

Timing

Intentionally Blank

Intentionally (almost) Blank

Please remember that we will be adding in what will be column (II) (c) later — It starts on the next page!

Guidance for Question A

There now follow *the rCs which are relevant to answering Question A.* As before, I am simply telling you the ones that are relevant. You will do more work later on all the *rCs* in the Handbook which are on the syllabus.

As a reminder, and for your convenience, here again is the outline of the first two rows of the headings of the Rubric Planning Template, this time with *column (II) (c)* added in.

Identify the Issue	*Describe the relevant parts of the syllabus*			*Explain with reference to the contents of the scenario*	*Advise resolve*
(i) Identify ethical issues. *State them generically*	(ii)(a) set out the relevant bits of the syllabus i.e. • **Syllabus Area 1;** ○ Relevant section of the Handbook ○ ~~Part 1,~~ 2 conduct rules, ~~3, 4 or 6?~~ ○ ~~Equality Rules?~~ • ~~any of syllabus Areas 2, 3 and 4?~~	(II)(B) CDS	(II)(C) rCs	(iii) apply your knowledge with a reasoned explanation of breach/no breach	(iv) *Resolve i.e. advise*

From here, just to gain some space, we are concentrating for the time being on just columns (ii) (a) (b) and (c).

<u>Do please remember that columns (i), (iii) and (iv) need to be included in your answer too.</u>

105

Guidance for Question A

Describe the relevant parts of the syllabus		
(ii)(a) Syllabus Part 1; ○ *Relevant parts of the Handbook –* *Part 2, Conduct Rules*	*(ii)(b)* CDS	*(ii)(c)* gCs *(Remember the numbering is not needed, it is included here just for teaching and practising purposes.)*
1. Indep in interests of justice; not comp	(CD4 CD1)	gC16 how public sees Barrister's conduct. gC14 Indep is fundamental. Keep indep from external pressures to resolve CD1 and CD2 conflict
2. Indep, not undermine	CD5	gC16 If public could think it undermined, could diminish their trust and confidence.
3. Pers resp, Own pj; justify d and a. nwt others		gC64 confirms this
	4. CD4 5. CD1 6. CD5	
1) Best int of each cl 2) Comp work	(CD2 CD7) 3) CD2 4) CD7 +SERV [99]	

---
[99] There are no relevant pieces of *guidance* for this part of the question.

106

Guidance for Question A

Now we are ready to give a full answer to the First Issue in Question A, by adding in the *CDs* to our previous answer. Here it is.

ANSWER TO QUESTION A

(i) *First Issue - Doing as my clerk suggests*

(ii) a) Handbook rules
1. A barrister must act with independence in the interests of justice. That independence should not be compromised. [100]

(ii) c) *Independence is fundamental.* [101] *I should keep independent from external pressures to resolve CD1 and CD2 conflict. There is no conflict between CD1 and CD2 in this question.* [102]

(iii) *Application*
It would be a breach of these rules if I blindly do as C says and take my planning to do on the plane as I would not be acting independently.

(iv) *Resolution*
I must make my own independent decision.

(ii) a) Handbook rules
2. I must not allow my independence to be undermined

c) *There is also guidance about the public's perception of a barrister's independence which I will refer to below in respect of Core Duty 5.*

(iii) *Application*
Taking the advice from my clerk to do my planning on the plane would undermine my independence and would be a breach of this rule.

---

[100] Another reason for separating the CDs we were prompted with through the rules prevents you from perhaps only having time in the assessment to set out what is in columns (ii)(a) (ii) (b) and (ii)(c). This could be disastrous, as if you run out of time, you will not have covered application and resolution from columns (iii) and (iv) of your Rubric Planning Template.

[101] Independence is more likely to raise its head in an assessment and in real life as set out in *CDs 18, 19 and 20.*

[102] There would be conflict between CD1 and CD2 if your client felt it would be in their best interests to, say, withhold new information from the court. You will learn how this conflict is resolved in the Second "Half" of this book, in the section YOU AND YOUR CLIENT.

Guidance for Question A

(iv) <u>Resolution</u>
I must make my own independent decision.

(ii) a) Handbook rules
3. A barrister
b) is personally responsible- **there is also guidance that confirms this**; must use their own professional judgment; and be able to justify their decisions and actions, notwithstanding the views of others.

(iii) *Application*
It would be a breach of this rule to take the clerk's advice without using my own professional judgment. I must decide what I decide notwithstanding her advice. Paring down 2 days' preparation to a couple of hours on a busy plane on my clerk's advice alone would mean that my client and the court were not best served by such a shortcut. Planning on a busy plane would be hard to justify.

(iv) <u>Resolution</u>
I must make my own independent decision.

(II) (B) <u>CORE DUTIES</u>

CD1 STATES THAT "YOU MUST OBSERVE YOUR DUTY TO THE COURT IN THE ADMINISTRATION OF JUSTICE."

(iii) *Application*
It would be a breach of this CD as I would not be observing my duty to the court if I did not prepare as fully as I should.

(iv) <u>Resolution</u>
I must prepare as fully and professionally as I can.

(II) (B) 5. CD4 STATES THAT "YOU MUST MAINTAIN YOUR INDEPENDENCE".

(iii) *Application*
Following my clerk's suggestion would be breach of CD4 because I must make my own professional decisions independently of anyone else.

(iv) <u>Resolution</u>
I must make my own independent decision

108

Guidance for Question A

(ii)   (B) 6. CD 5 STATES THAT "YOU MUST NOT BEHAVE IN A WAY WHICH IS LIKELY TO DIMINISH THE TRUST AND CONFIDENCE WHICH THE PUBLIC PLACES IN YOU OR IN THE PROFESSION."

(ii)   (c) There is guidance which states that if the public could think that a barrister's independence has been undermined, then that could diminish their trust and confidence in the profession

Application

(iii)   The solicitors and their clients who would have heard my clerk saying that I should cut down my planning time to do it on the plane could have had their trust and confidence in the profession diminished, if they believed that I, a barrister, would be providing an ill prepared service to my client. The same could be true of fellow plane passengers who saw what I was doing.

(iv)   *Resolution*

Had I responded there and then that I would not be paring down my preparation that would have avoided a breach. I must remember in future to avoid any conversations in a public area that could result in that breach. I will remind my clerk of this. Since I will not be going to Prague and will prepare fully over two days I have made the correct decision.

Second Issue – Taking less time to plan

You will remember from the footnote at the bottom of the latest table that there is no additional guidance to add, so your answer will remain the same as you did yourself earlier, just with shorter headings and perhaps the CDs separated out from the rules that prompted them.

You may wish to have a go at writing out your sleeker version of this second issue on the next page.

Intentionally Blank

Hint Seven

Make every word count

You may be interested to know that on a word count analysis of our answers to Question A, that when added together,

- ❖ our first long hand answer, the one where it was all rolled up into one issue, before we had added in the *guidance,* the one which began

    "The ethical issue which arises is potentially not preparing fully for a court appearance.

    - Describe relevant parts of the ethics syllabus"

and

- ❖ our most recent sleeker answer, for the First Issue, contracting down the headings, yet writing more content in our answer because we had separated out the rules and guidance from the CDs, to allow us to fulfil columns (ii) and (iv) of the Rubric Planning Template, and then adding on the wordcount from our first long hand answer for the second issue, the one which began

    "ANSWER TO QUESTION A

    (i) First Issue - Doing as my clerk suggests"

total about the same word count. The difference is that the final most recent version contains more mark – hitting content.

That leads us neatly onto Hint Eight on the next page.

Hint Eight

Make every second count

You really do have to focus, keep your head down, think quickly, yet keep a cool head in the assessment in the form that you will be sitting it in 2020. There is no spare time at all.

<u>An important reminder on Timing.</u>

Remember that for each 10 mark question, we have been hypothesising 12 minutes to plan and 12 minutes to write.

Therefore, you have just 12 minutes to plan both parts a) and b) and 12 minutes to write out both parts a) and b).

For a 2 part question of 5 marks each, that's

6 minutes plan, 6 minutes write

6 minutes plan, 6 minutes write

For a 2 part question of 6 marks and 4 marks, that's

5 minutes plan, 5 minutes write

8 minutes plan, 7 minutes write

For a 2 part question of 8 marks and 2 marks, that's

10 minutes plan, 9 minutes write

3 minutes plan, 3 minutes write

So let's imagine that our Question A had been presented in such a way that it was a 2 part question of 8 marks and 2 marks.

A possible mark scheme for Question A

ANSWER TO QUESTION A

a) **(maximum 8 marks)**

Issue - Doing as my clerk suggests *(1/2)*;

Handbook rules and guidance

- A barrister must act with independence in the interests of justice. *(1/2)*;

  That independence should not be compromised. *(1/2)*; [It may be that you only get these marks if you have applied them as in the next paragraphs].

  It would be a breach of these rules if I blindly do as my clerk says and take my planning to do on the plane as I would not be acting independently in reaching my decision. *(1/2)*;

  Independence is fundamental. [103]I should keep independent from external pressures to resolve CD1 and CD2 conflict. There is no conflict between Cd1 and CD2 in this question, *(1/2)*;[104]

  I must make my own independent decision *(1/2)*;

- I must not allow my independence to be undermined. *(1/2)*; There is also guidance about the public's perception of a barrister's independence *(1/2)*; which I will refer to below in respect of Core Duty 5. [It may be that you only get these marks if you have applied them as in the next paragraphs].

  Taking the advice from my clerk to do my planning on the plane would undermine my independence and would be a breach of these rules. *(1/2)*;

  I must make my own independent decision. *(1/2)*;

- A barrister is personally responsible *(1/2)*;– there is guidance that confirms this; *(1/2)*; Barristers must use their own professional judgment *(1/2)*;, and be able to justify their decisions and actions, notwithstanding the views of others. *(1/2)*; [It may be that you only get these marks if you have applied them as in the next paragraphs].

  It would be a breach of this rule to take the clerk's advice without using my own professional judgment. I must decide what I decide notwithstanding her advice. Paring down 2 days' preparation to a couple of hours on a busy plane on my clerk's advice alone would mean that my client and the court were not best served by such a shortcut. Planning on a busy plane would be hard to justify. *(1/2)*;

  I must make my own independent decision. *(1/2)*;

---

[103] Independence is more likely to raise its head in an assessment as set out in *cCs 18, 19 and 20*.
[104] There would be conflict between *CD1* and *CD2* if your client felt it would be in their best interests to, say, withhold new information from the court. You will learn how this conflict is resolved in the Second "Half" of this book.

A possible mark scheme for Question A

Core Duties

- CD1 states that "you must observe your duty to the court in the administration of justice." *(1/2)*; [It may be that you only get these marks if you have applied them as in the next paragraphs].

    It would be a breach of this CD as I would not be observing my duty to the court if I did not prepare as fully as I should. *(1/2)*;

    I must prepare as fully and professionally as I can. *(1/2)*;

- CD4 states that "you must maintain your independence". *(1/2)*; [It may be that you only get these marks if you have applied them as in the next paragraphs].

    Following blindly my clerk's suggestion to prepare on the plane would be breach of CD4 because I must make my own professional decisions independently of anyone else. *(1/2)*;

    I must make my own independent decision. *(1/2)*;

- CD 5 states that "you must not behave in a way which is likely to diminish the trust and confidence which the public places in you or in the profession." *(1/2)*; [It may be that you only get these marks if you have applied them as in the next paragraphs].

    There is guidance which states that if the public could think that a barrister's independence has been undermined, then that could diminish their trust and confidence in the profession. *(1/2)*;

    The solicitors and their clients who would have heard my clerk saying that I should cut down my planning time to do it on the plane could have had their trust and confidence in the profession diminished, if they believed that I, a barrister, would be providing an ill prepared service to my client. The same could be true of fellow plane passengers who saw what I was doing. *(1/2)*;

    Had I responded there and then that I would not be paring down my preparation that would have avoided a breach. *(1/2)*; I must remember in future to avoid any conversations in a public area that could result in that breach. *(1/2)*; I will remind my clerk of this. *(1/2)*; Since I will not be going to Prague and will prepare fully over two days I have made the correct decision.

A possible mark scheme for Question A

b) **(maximum 2 marks)**[105]

Column (i) Issue – Taking less time to plan *(1/2);*

Columns (ii) (a) (b) and (c)

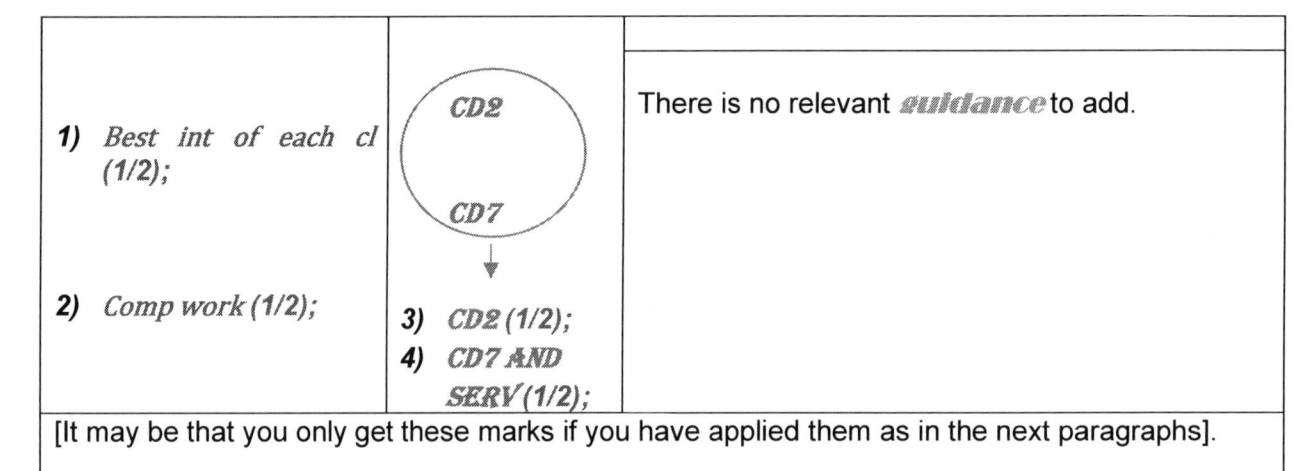

1) Best int of each cl *(1/2);*	CD2 CD7 ↓	There is no relevant *guidance* to add.
2) *Comp work (1/2);*	3) *CD2 (1/2);* 4) *CD7 AND SERV (1/2);*	
[It may be that you only get these marks if you have applied them as in the next paragraphs].		

Column (iii)

Plus for column (iii) application for each of the 4 elements in column (ii) as follows

1) and 3) will be the same, so a maximum of *(1/2)* for correct application.

2) and 4) will be the same, so a maximum of *(1/2)* for correct application.

Column (iv)

Plus for column (iv), resolution for each of the 4 points *(1/2) each;*

Further observations on Question A and the possible mark schemes.

Please be aware that this question and suggested mark scheme have not been through the rigorous processes that will be the case for the actual assessment questions. They are, though, as close a representation as possible for illustrative purposes, of assessment questions and mark schemes.

The way that the mark scheme above for the First Issue is set out, is the way that mark schemes have so far been presented for the formative/mock assessments and for both of the 2017 assessments.

An assessment question is more likely to be divided into a least two parts, rather than in one large part, as Question A has been presented.

---

[105] We have not included, neither as an issue nor in the answer, any reference to reporting serious misconduct of others, prompted by the clerk's comment about working on the plane, given her later statement that it was a long time ago, different chambers.

A possible mark scheme for Question A

When using the suggested mark scheme above, the First Issue would likely attract a maximum of 8 marks and the Second Issue a maximum of 2 marks. (This is an unusual split, though).

Do remember that you are required to apply the rules and principles (i.e. the contents of column (iii)) and that if you do not, you may not be awarded marks for what you have written from your columns (ii) (a) (b) and (c). Remember to do the column (iv) resolution as well.

Intentionally Blank

THE SECOND "HALF"

SELECTING FROM THE SYLLABUS
THE CONTENTS
OF COLUMNS (II) (A) (B) (C)
FOR YOUR ANSWER

Intentionally Blank

YOU AND THE COURT
Rules and *CORE DUTIES*

You will recall that in answering Question A in the First "Half", you were given the correct parts of the syllabus to include in your answer.

Now we are going to work on learning the contents of the syllabus, revisiting those areas of the syllabus that you have already met whilst doing question A, then now adding in the remainder of those *Conduct Rules* which were not relevant to Question A.

In the spirit of incremental learning, we will start with just the *Rules,* (and hence also the mapped-on *CORE DUTIES*). Once you become familiar with those, the *guidance* will be mapped on in turn.

We start with what you have met before. If you have been a model student, you will have already committed to memory

<u>*Section C - The Conduct Rules*</u>

YOU AND THE COURT

BEHAVING ETHICALLY

YOU AND YOUR CLIENT

YOU AND YOUR REGULATOR

YOU AND YOUR PRACTICE

↓

<u>*The Conduct Rules*</u>

<u>*YOU AND THE COURT*</u> *CD 1*

- *Independence in the interests of justice* *CD 4*
- *Not misleading the court*
- *Not abusing your role as an advocate*

<u>*BEHAVING ETHICALLY*</u>

- *Honesty, integrity and independence* *CD 3 AND 4 AND 5*
  5
- *Referral fees*
- *Undertakings*
- *Discrimination*
- *Foreign work*

<u>*YOU AND YOUR CLIENT*</u>

- *Best interests of each client,* *CD 2*
  provision of a competent standard of work *CD 7*
  and confidentiality
- *Not misleading potential clients*
- *Personal responsibility* *CD 4*
- *Accepting Instructions*
- *Defining terms or basis on which instructions are accepted*

YOU AND THE COURT
Rules and *CORE DUTIES*

- *Returning instructions*
- *Requirement not to discriminate*
- *The 'cab-rank' rule*

YOU AND YOUR REGULATOR

- *Provision of information to the Bar Standards Board*
- *Duty to report certain matters to the Bar Standards Board*
- *Reporting serious misconduct by others*
- *Access to premises*
- *Co-operation with the Legal Ombudsman*
- *Ceasing to Practice*

YOU AND YOUR PRACTICE

- *Client money*
- *Insurance*
- *Associations with others*
- *Outsourcing*
- *Administration and conduct of self-employed practice*

Next we are fleshing out the three main headings in *YOU AND THE COURT.*

YOU AND THE COURT
Rules and *CORE DUTIES*

THE FULL CONTENTS OF THE *RULES* ON
INDEPENDENCE IN THE INTERESTS OF JUSTICE (rCS 3-5)

Please note that the *rCs* are greatly contracted in this book in an effort to make committing them to memory less daunting. You should refer to the actual *rCs* in the Handbook yourself, to be sure that you fully understand the full meaning behind these contracted versions.

- *Not knowingly or recklessly mislead the court* – see more detail overleaf.
- *Not abuse role as advocate* – see more detail overleaf.
- *Not waste court time*
- *Ensure court has decisions and law*
- *Ensure independence is not compromised*

Duty to court / best interests of each client; i.e. CD1 / CD2; ie. The "fraction" 1 / 2
Confidentiality to client / duty to court; i.e. CD6 / CD1 ; i.e. the "fraction" 6 /1

Remember that now is a good point in your learning to map the relevant *CORE DUTIES* on to the rules. Here they will be
- Independence in the interests of justice *CD4*
- Also *CD1, CD2 AND CD6,* given their overt inclusion in this section.

So for answers where you have decided that the relevant area of the Handbook to use in your answer is *YOU AND THE COURT,* you should also be alert to the need also to address *CDS 1, 2, 4 AND 6* in your answer.

So column (ii) of a Rubric Planning Template for *YOU AND THE COURT,* so far now looks like this:-

	(ii) (a)		(ii) (b)
YOU AND THE COURT	*Independence in the interests of justice* [106]	• Not mislead court[109] • Not abuse role [110] • Not waste court time • Ensure decisions and law • Indep not comp	CD4 [111]
	CD1/CD2 [107] *CD6/CD1* [108]		CD1 CD2 Y CD6

---

[106] *rC3* Remember that you do not need to know the numbering, they simply here to help you navigate the Handbook.
[107] *rC4*
[108] *rC5*
[109] Has its own section as *rC6* – see more detail overleaf.
[110] Has its own section as *rC7* – see more detail overleaf
[111] I have now dropped the reference to CD1 here as it arises more naturally in the overt reference to it in *rC4*

YOU AND THE COURT
Rules and *CORE DUTIES*

THE FULL CONTENTS OF THE *RULES* ON

NOT MISLEADING THE COURT (rC6)

Includes

- *No untrue/misleading submissions or questions*
- *Can call Witness re untrue/misleading if you tell the court*

So column (ii) of Rubric Planning Template for YOU AND THE COURT, so far looks like this, with the firsr row as created above now shaded so you can concentrate on the new content:-

	(ii) (a)		(ii) (b)
YOU AND THE COURT	*Independence in the interests of justice* CD1/CD2 CD6/CD1	• *Not mislead* • *Not abuse role* • *Not waste court time* • *Ensure decisions and law* • *Indep not comp*	CD4 CD1 CD2 CD6
	Not mislead the court	*Includes* • *No untrue/misleading submissions or questions suggesting facts to W. i.e Barrister cannot say it* • *Can call W re untrue/misleading if you tell the court. i,e, Witness cannot say it*	

THE FULL CONTENTS OF THE *RULES* ON

NOT ABUSING YOUR ROLE AS AN ADVOCATE (rC7)

Includes

- *Not insult anyone*
- *Only make serious alleg v W if they've had a chance to answer it in your XX*
- *Not make serious alleg nor accuse other re your cl's charged crime without*
  - *Reasonable grounds +*
  - *Rel to cl's case or W credibility +*
  - *Not name 3rd pty in open ct unless reasonably nec*
- *Not give own opinion unless ct/law asks*

YOU AND THE COURT
Rules and *CORE DUTIES*

So column (ii) of Rubric Planning Template for the *rules* in *YOU AND THE COURT*, with relevant *CDS* mapped on, awaiting the addition of the *guidance* looks like this

	(ii) (a)		(II) (B)
YOU AND THE COURT	*Independence in the interests of justice* CD1/CD2 CD6/CD1	• Not mislead • Not abuse role • Not waste court time • Ensure decisions and law • Indep not comp	CD4 CD1 CD2 CD6
	Not mislead the court	*Includes* • *No untrue/misleading submissions or questions* • *Can call W re untrue/misleading if you tell the court*	

	Not abusing your role as an advocate	*Includes*
		• *Not insult anyone*
		• *Only make serious alleg v W if they've had a chance to answer it in your XX*
		• *Not make serious alleg v any person Nor accuse other re your cl's charged crime without*
		    ○ *Reasonable grounds +*
		    ○ *Rel to cl's case or W credibility +*
		    ○ *Not name 3rd pty in open ct unless reasonably nec*
		• *Not give own opinion unless ct/law asks*
			CD3 + CD5

Intentionally Blank

Next we are fleshing out in the same way, the five main headings in

BEHAVING ETHICALLY (rCs8- 14)

THE FULL CONTENTS OF THE *RULES* ON

HONESTY, INTEGRITY AND INDEPENDENCE

- *Do not undermine*
- *CD3 –*
  - *not mislead (attempt) anyone* [112]
  - *not draft docs unless*
    - *cl supports or instructs*
    - *it is properly arguable*
    - *clear instruction and creditably arguable re fraud*
    - *W statement is what cl would say orally*
- *Not encourage W to give untruthful / misleading*
- *Not rehearse W re evidence*
- *Not communicate with W whilst they give evidence unless other side permission*
- *Not pay W re evidence / outcome*
- *Only legal fees*

THE FULL CONTENTS OF THE *RULES* ON
REFERRAL FEES

No, cannot do it.

THE FULL CONTENTS OF THE *RULES* ON
UNDERTAKINGS

Comply as agreed or in a reasonable period

THE FULL CONTENTS OF THE *RULES* ON

DISCRIMINATION

Not victimise or harass re all things discrim

THE FULL CONTENTS OF THE *RULES* ON

FOREIGN WORK

- *Unless not consistent with CDs*
  - *Comply where it is / proceedings are / contemplated*
- *Soliciting work, do it as per the outside jurisdiction of the local Bar*

So column (ii) of Rubric Planning Template for the *rules* in *BEHAVING ETHICALLY*, with relevant *CDS* mapped on, awaiting the addition of the *guidance* looks like this:

---

[112] Notice that in *YOU AND THE COURT* it is the <u>court</u> that must not be mislead; in *BEHAVING ETHICALLY* it is <u>anyone</u> that you must not mislead

BEHAVING ETHICALLY (rCs8- 14)

BEHAVING ETHICALLY	Honesty, integrity and independence	<ul><li>Do not undermine</li><li>CD3 –<ul><li>not mislead (attempt) anyone [113]</li><li>not draft docs unless<ul><li>cl supports or instructs</li><li>it is properly arguable</li><li>clear instruction and creditably arguable re fraud</li><li>W statement is what cl would say orally</li></ul></li></ul></li><li>Not encourage W to give untruthful / misleading</li><li>Not rehearse W re evidence</li><li>Not communicate with W whilst they give evidence unless other side permission</li><li>Not pay W re evidence / outcome</li><li>Only legal fees</li></ul>	CDS3 AND 4 CD5 IF THE PUBLIC HAVE WITNESSED DISHONESTY, LACK OF INTEGRITY OR LACK OF INDEPENDENCE
	Referral fees	No	
	Undertakings	Comply as agreed or in a reasonable period	
	Discrimination	Not victimise or harass re all things discrim	CD8
	Foreign work	<ul><li>Unless not consistent with CDs<ul><li>Comply where it is / proceedings are / contemplated</li></ul></li><li>Soliciting work, do it as per the outside jurisdiction of the local Bar</li></ul>	

---

[113] Notice that in *YOU AND THE COURT* it is the court that must not be misled; in *BEHAVING ETHICALLY* it is anyone that you must not mislead

YOU AND YOUR CLIENT
Rules and *CORE DUTIES*

Next, without the need for setting out the full content first, by now, is the similar template for
YOU AND YOUR CLIENT.

YOU AND YOUR CLIENT	• Best interests of each [114] client	Best inte?rests duty includes if cl best served by different legal rep + inform cl of this	*CD2*
	• Competent standard of work	This incl duty to tell (sol/lay) cl asap if — Apparent can't do it in time / in reasonable time — any risk of this	*CD7*

	• Confidentiality	All 3 read as if to include
		• Fearlessly and lawfully promote cl's best interests
		• No regard to own interests / consequences – mitigate any breach
		• No regard to consequences for others
		• Not allow anyone to limit yr discretion re serving clients' interests
		• Protect the confidentiality of each cl except
		  ○ Req'd/permitted by law
		  ○ Cl gives informed consent
			CD6
			
			6/1 "*FRACTION*"

	CD 1/2 CD 3/2 CD 4/2		*CD1* *CD3* *CD4*
	Not misleading clients or potential clients [115]	Not mislead/cause/permit who you supply to/offer to re • Nature and scope of legal services • Terms/who do it/basis of charging • Who legally responsible • Entitled to perform/regulated • Any insurance for Prof Neg	*CD3* *CD5* [116]
	Personal Responsibility	Notwithstanding views of others, use own prof judgment be able to justify decisions and actions	*CD4*

---

[114] So you need to consider both clients if there are two of them. Considering the interests of EACH
[115] Note that this is the third reference to misleading – be sure to choose the one(s) that best fit your scenario.
[116] CD5, here, is the author's suggestion. It is not overtly set out in the Handbook at this point.

YOU AND YOUR CLIENT
Rules and *CORE DUTIES*

Although the next section of the Handbook deals with *Accepting Instructions* I and the students I worked with, felt that it helped memorise the syllabus in what we agreed was a more logical order by introducing the 'cab-rank' Rule next. This is because the 'cab-rank' Rule begins with when you DO accept instructions and then sets out when the 'cab-rank' rule does not apply; whereas the section called *Accepting Instructions* deals with when you MUST NOT accept instructions.

Activity

Please take some time now to complete the following template using the contents of *rC29 and rC30*.

(You can leave the *guidance* until later.)

THE 'CAB-RANK' RULE (rC29-30)

	(ii) (a)		(II) (B)
YOU AND YOUR CLIENT	The 'Cab-rank' rule	• Must accept *Irrespective of*	
		• Does not apply if	

YOU AND YOUR CLIENT
Rules and *CORE DUTIES*

ACCEPTING INSTRUCTIONS (rC 21)

Activity

Please take some time now to refer back to a previous activity where you filled in the 10 elements on when not to accept instructions.

You can then complete the following column (ii) (a) template for that.

The first relevant *CD* is copied into column *(II) (B)*.

Do remember to include as well, the other relevant *CDS* for this *rule* in column *(II) (B)*.

		(ii)　　(a)	(II)　　(B)
YOU AND YOUR CLIENT	Accepting Instructions	• No if 1 2 3 4 5 6 7 8 9 10	?CD2

132

YOU AND YOUR CLIENT
Rules and CORE DUTIES

DEFINING TERMS OR BASIS ON WHICH INSTRUCTIONS ARE ACCEPTED (rC 22-24)

	(ii) (a)		*(II)*	*(B)*
YOU AND YOUR CLIENT	*Defining terms or basis on which instructions are accepted*	• *Confirm acceptance in writing +terms + basis of charging* ○ *To sol if instr by sol* ○ *To cl. If intsr by cl.* ○ *If BSB auth'd body get cl consent to disclose+give control of files to BSB or agent where terms of auth to practise not met* *[these terms not on syllabus]* • *No need to do it again re varied/additional instructions as deemed accepted on same terms as when you began the work, unless specified otherwise* • *Must comply with these 2 bullet points before doing the work* *Unless* *not reasonably practicable; so do it as soon as it is reasonably practicable.*		

YOU AND YOUR CLIENT
Rules and *CORE DUTIES*

RETURNING INSTRUCTIONS (rC 25-27)

	(ii) (a)	(II) (B)

YOU AND YOUR CLIENT	Returning Instructions	**MUST Cease to act and return** if
		
		○ Have started but any one of the 10 above re not accepting arises. PROMPTLY return
		
		○ Legal aid/crim funding wrongly obtained and cl does not remedy it immediately
		
		○ Cl refuses to allow you to disclose something to court
		
		○ Another is
		   ○ Become aware of doc should have been but was not disclosed
		   ○ You advise cl they need to disclose it and they don't/won't let you
			CD1
			CD2 [117]

		MAY cease to act and return if ○ Your prof conduct called into question; OR ○ Cl consents; OR ○ You are self employed or a BSB authorised body PLUS ○ Prof diary already has something in it where hearing on that date and reasonable efforts to prevent it OR ○ Ill/pregnancy/childbirth/bereavement /similar prevents ○ You are unavoidably on jury service • You are not paid when due • Aware, re what you are instructed on, of ○ confidential docs/priv'd info ○ docs of another	CD3

---

[117] *CD2* has been added here because you sometimes need to state in an answer that there is no breach of *CD2* where what the client may see as in their best interests would mean a breach of Professional Ethics, e.g. of *CD1*. In this case you need to explain to your client the "fraction" ½ in *column (iv)* of your Rubric Planning Template.

		<ul><li>*in litig +*
		  ○ *cl not consent to ceasing to act; or*
		  ○ *your application to come off the record has been granted*</li><li>*SOME OTHER SUBSTANTIAL REASON*</li></ul>	

		All - i.e. both the MUST and MAY ceasing to act and returning instructions - subject to<ul><li>*Getting cl consent or explain reason for ceasing to act to cl*</li><li>*Not being discrim re*
		  ❖ *It being objectionable to you/public*
		  ❖ *Cl conduct, opinions, beliefs, objectionable to you/public*</li></ul>*Source of finance properly to be given to prospective cl for the proceedings*
			CD8

Intentionally Blank

Guidance
CORE DUTIES

Guidance

This section of this book deals with the *guidance* in the Handbook.

The first set of *guidance* is given in relation to the *CORE DUTIES*.

This is a very short section, some of which is repeated later on in the *rules* in the Handbook in the sections *YOU AND THE COURT* and *YOU AND YOUR CLIENT*.

It is therefore only that guidance that is not repeated later (in fact you have already come across the repetitions!) that we will enter here at this point.

That is *CD8 / CD2. 8/2*

Also *CD10 includes an obligation to take all reasonable steps to mitigate the effects of any breach of those legal and regulatory obligations once you become aware of them. CD10*

You may find it useful to go back to the list of *CORE DUTIES* that you faithfully copied into this book towards the beginning, in order to add this piece of guidance to *CDS 8, 2 AND 10.*

Guidance
YOU AND THE COURT
Intentionally Blank

Guidance
YOU AND THE COURT

<u>The second set of *guidance* is given in relation to the *rules* of the Handbook</u>

We will start again with *YOU AND THE COURT.*

Remember that for your Rubric Planning Template, we have put *the rules in Column (ii) (a), the CDs in column (ii) (b);* now we will be adding in the *guidance in column (ii) (c).*

To achieve this you will need to read the following pages across both pages, where columns *(ii) (a)* and *(ii) (b)* are on the left hand page and column *(ii) (c)* is on the right hand page.

YOU AND THE COURT
Guidance

	(ii) (a)		(II) (B)
YOU AND THE COURT	Independence in the interests of justice	• Not mislead ct • Not abuse role • Not waste court time • Ensure decisions and law • Indep not comp	CD4
	CD1/CD2		CD1 CD2
	CD6/CD1		CD6
	Not mislead the court	Includes • No untrue/misleading submissions or questions • Can call W re untrue/misleading if you tell the court	
	Not abusing your role as an advocate	As earlier – no *guidance* on this rule. So omitted here, to save space.	CD3 + CD5

140

	(ii) (c)
Not mislead ct	knowingly = inadvertently, realise, fail to correct recklessly = indifference, not caring if true/false [gC4]. See also further in this template.
Not waste ct time	• Tell ct of decision/provision adverse to your cl's interests, especially re litigant in person. [gC5] • If you aware cl has doc that should disclose but hasn't, only cont to act if cl agrees to disclose it; if not, you cannot reveal existence or contents to ct. [118] [gCs9 and 13] CD6
CD1/CD2 [119]	• compliance ensured e.g. where cl tells you he did commit the crime as CD6/CD1 [gC8]; need cl consent to disclose that info [gC9]; if cl refuses to allow you to disclose confid info, cease to act and return instructions [120]; you cannot reveal the confid info to ct.[gC11] [see further gC 12 re crim convictions] • 1/2 conflicts resolving gives rise to also 3/2 and 4/2 [gC14 [121]]
re CD1	No breach (even if you don't believe facts as cl states them) if you put the +ve case forward re your instructions AND do not mislead the ct. Not for barrister to decide whether cl case is to be believed. [gC6]
Not mislead ct	No breach if • call W to confirm statement if draw W's att'n to poss conflicting evidence, indicate to ct may find ev difficult to accept, yet W maintains it's true and that is recorded in WS [gC7] • you make it clear to ct when you call a hostile W whose evidence you are instructed is untrue [gC7] • cl tells you he did commit the crime yet entered not guilty plea then barrister tests in XX reliability of pros W evidence + address jury that pros not succeeded in making them sure of your cl's guilt [gC9] Breach if • set up +ve case inconsistent with the confession [gC10 gives examples

---

[118] Remember how this appears as a further rule in *YOU AND YOUR CLIENT* as the fourth in list of when you must return instructions
[119] Referring to the rule which states *CD1/CD2* in *rC4*
[120] Remember that *YOU AND YOUR CLIENT, Returning Instructions* sets out how to do this.
[121] Remember how this appears as a further rule in *YOU AND YOUR CLIENT* as *rC16*

Intentionally Blank

The next page is a distillation of the previous 2 pages onto one page.

YOU AND THE COURT

Rules CDS and *Guidance* all on one page

	(ii) (a)		(II) (B)	(II) (C)
YOU AND THE COURT	Independence in the interests of justice	• Not mislead • Not abuse role • Not waste court time • Ensure decisions and law • Indep not comp	CD4	gC4 gC5,9,13
	CD1/CD2		CD1 CD2	gC6 gC 8, 9,11, 12,14
	CD6/CD1		CD6	gC8,9,13
	Not mislead the court	Includes • No untrue/misleading submissions or questions • Can call W re untrue/misleading if you tell the court		gC7,9,10

	Not abusing your role as an advocate	Includes
		• Not insult anyone
		• Only make serious alleg v W if they've had a chance to answer you in XX
		• Not accuse other re your cl's crime without
		   ○ Reasonable grounds +
		   ○ Rel to cl's case or W credibility +
		   ○ Not name 3rd pty in open ct unless reasonably nec
		• Not give own opinion unless ct/law asks
			CD3 + CD5	

Intentionally Blank

In the next section, *BEHAVING ETHICALLY*, you could transcribe the *guidance* for *BEHAVING ETHICALLY* onto the righthand page; and on the page after that you could put all of *BEHAVING ETHICALLY* onto one page in the same way as we just did for *YOU AND THE COURT* - Do remember to add in the *guidance* in the final column

BEHAVING ETHICALLY
Guidance

	(ii) (a)		(II) (B)
BEHAVING ETHICALLY	Honesty, integrity and independence	<ul><li>Do not undermine</li><li>CD3 –<ul><li>not mislead (attempt) anyone</li><li>not draft docs unless<ul><li>cl supports or instructs</li><li>it is properly arguable</li><li>clear instruction and creditably arguable re fraud</li><li>W statement is what cl would say orally</li></ul></li></ul></li><li>Not encourage W to give untruthful</li><li>Not rehearse W re evidence</li><li>Not communicate with W whilst they give evidence unless other side permission</li><li>Not pay W re evidence / outcome</li><li>Only legal fees</li></ul>	CDS3 AND 4 CD5 IF THE PUBLIC HAVE WITNESSED DISHONESTY, LACK OF INTEGRITY OR LACK OF INDEPENDENCE
	Referral fees	No	
	Undertakings	Comply as agreed or in a reasonable period	
	Discrimination	Not victimise or harass re all things discrim	CD8
	Foreign work	<ul><li>Unless not consistent with CDs<ul><li>Comply where it is / proceedings are / contemplated</li></ul></li><li>Soliciting work, do it as per the outside jurisdiction of the local Bar</li></ul>	

BEHAVING ETHICALLY
Guidance

| (ii) | (c) [122] |

---
[122] Remember this is for you to complete, lined up alongside columns (ii) (a) and (ii) (b)

Intentionally Blank

BEHAVING ETHICALLY
Rules CDS and Guidance all on one page

		(ii) (a)	*(II)* (B)	*(ii)* (c)[123]

BEHAVING ETHICALLY	Honesty, integrity and independence	• Do not undermine
		• CD3 –
		  ○ not mislead (attempt) anyone
		  ○ not draft docs unless
		    ▪ cl supports or instructs
		    ▪ it is properly arguable
		    ▪ clear instruction and creditably arguable re fraud
		    ▪ W statement is what cl would say orally
		• Not encourage W to give untruthful
		• Not rehearse W re evidence
		• Not communicate with W whilst they give evidence unless other side permission
		• Not pay W re evidence / outcome
		• Only legal fees
			CDS3 AND 4
			
			CD5 IF THE PUBLIC HAVE WITNESSED DISHONESTY, LACK OF INTEGRITY OR LACK OF INDEPENDENCE	

	Referral fees	No		
	Undertakings	Comply as agreed or in a reasonable period		
	Discrimination	Not victimise or harass re all things discrim	CD8	
	Foreign work	• Unless not consistent with CDs ○ Comply where it is / proceedings are / contemplated • Soliciting work, do it as per the outside jurisdiction of the local Bar		

---

[123] Remember that you need to fill in this column

BEHAVING ETHICALLY
Rules CDS and Guidance all on one page

Intentionally Blank

YOU AND YOUR CLIENT
Guidance first page

Please be aware that the following pages do continue in the same mode;

the lefthand page is columns (ii) (a) and (ii) (b),

the righthand page is column (ii) (c) for you to fill in the guidance reading across from (ii) (a) and (ii) (b)

the final page of the section is for you to fit it all onto one page as you have done with previous sections.

The only difference this time is that the smallest of pitch size will not get this legibly onto one page. Therefore the top right hand side of each page indicates whether you are dealing with the first or second page of the same section.

YOU AND YOUR CLIENT
Guidance first page

	(ii) (a)	(ii) (a)	(II) (C)
YOU AND YOUR CLIENT	• Best interests of each [124] client	Best interests duty includes if cl best served by different legal rep + inform cl of this	CD2
	• Competent standard of work and service	This incl duty to tell (sol/lay)cl asap if — Apparent can't do it in time / in reasonable time — any risk of this	CD7

	• Confidentiality	All 3 read as if to include
		• Fearlessly and lawfully promote cl's best interests
		• No regard to own interests / consequences – mitigate any breach
		• No regard to consequences for others
		• Not allow anyone to limit yr discretion re serving clients' interests
		• Protect the confidentiality of each cl except
		  ○ Req'd/permitted by law
		  ○ Cl gives informed consent
			CD6
			
			6/1
			"FRACTION"

	CD 1/2 CD 3/2 CD 4/2		CD1 CD3 CD4
	Guidance also adds in CD8/CD2		CD8/CD2
	Not misleading clients or potential clients [125]	Not mislead/cause/permit who you supply to/offer to re • Nature and scope of legal services • Terms/who do it/basis of charging • Who legally responsible • Entitled to perform/regulated • Any insurance for Prof Neg	CD3 CD5
	Personal Responsibility	Notwithstanding views of others, use own prof judgment be able to justify decisions and actions	CD4

---

[124] So you need to consider both clients if there are two of them. Considering the interests of each
[125] Note that this is the third reference to misleading – be sure to choose the one(s) that best fit your scenario.

YOU AND YOUR CLIENT
Guidance first page
Intentionally Blank for *column (II) (c)*

Intentionally Blank

YOU AND YOUR CLIENT
Guidance first page
Rules, CDS and Guidance all on one page

	(ii) (a)	(ii) (a)	(II) (B)	(ii) (C) [127]

YOU AND YOUR CLIENT	• Best interests of each [126] client
	
	• Competent standard of work and service
	
	• Confidentiality
	
	CD 1/2
	CD 3/2
	CD 4/2
	
	Guidance also adds in CD8/CD2
		Best interests duty includes if cl best served by different legal rep + inform cl of this
		
		This incl duty to tell (sol/lay)cl asap if
		..... Apparent can't do it in time / in reasonable time
		..... any risk of this
		
		All 3 can be read to include
		• Fearlessly and lawfully promote cl's best interests
		• No regard to own interests / consequences – mitigate any breach
		• No regard to consequences for others
		• Not allow anyone to limit yr discretion re serving clients' interests
		• Protect the confidentiality of each cl except
		  ◦ Req'd/permitted by law
		  ◦ Cl gives informed consent
			CD2
			
			CD7
			
			CD6
			
			6/1 "FRACTION"
			
			CD1
			CD3
			CD4
			
			CD8/CD2	

	Not misleading clients or potential clients [128]	Not mislead/cause/permit who you supply to/offer to re • Nature and scope of legal services • Terms/who do it/basis of charging • Who legally responsible • Entitled to perform/regulated • Any insurance for Prof Neg	CD3 CD5	
	Personal Responsibility	Notwithstanding views of others, use own prof judgment be able to justify decisions and actions	CD4	

---

[126] So you need to consider both clients if there are two of them. Considering the interests of each
[127] Remember that this is for you to fill in
[128] Note that this is the third reference to misleading – be sure to choose the one(s) that best fit your scenario.

Intentionally Blank

Intentionally Blank

YOU AND YOUR CLIENT
Guidance second page

| YOU AND YOUR CLIENT | (ii) (a)

The Cab-rank rule | (ii) (a)

• Must accept

Irrespective of

• Does not apply if | (II) (B) |

YOU AND YOUR CLIENT
Guidance second page
Column (II) (c)

Intentionally Blank

YOU AND YOUR CLIENT
Rules, CDs and *Guidance second page* all on one page

YOU AND YOUR CLIENT	(ii) (a) The 'Cab-rank' rule	(ii) (a) • Must accept Irrespective of	(II) (B)	(II) (C)
		• Does not apply if		

Intentionally Blank

Intentionally Blank

YOU AND YOUR CLIENT
Guidance third page

YOU AND YOUR CLIENT	(ii) (a) Accepting Instructions	(ii) (b)	(II) (C)
		• No if 1 2 3 4 5 6 7 8 9 10	CD2
	Defining terms or basis on which instructions are accepted	• Confirm acceptance in writing +terms + basis of charging ○ To sol if instr by sol ○ To cl. If intsr by cl. ○ If BSB auth'd body get cl consent to disclose+give control of files to BSB or agent where terms of auth to practise not met [these terms not on syllabus] • No need to do it again re varied/additional instructions as deemed accepted on same terms as when you began the work, unless specified otherwise • Must comply with these 2 bullet points before doing the work Unless not reasonably practicable; so do it as soon as it is reasonably practicable.	

YOU AND YOUR CLIENT
Guidance third page
Column (ii) (c)

Intentionally Blank

YOU AND YOUR CLIENT
Rules, CDS and *Guidance third page* all on one page

YOU AND YOUR CLIENT	(ii) (a) Accepting Instructions	(ii) (a)	(II) (B)	(iii) (C)
		• No if 1 2 3 4 5 6 7 8 9 10	CD2	
	Defining terms or basis on which instructions are accepted	• Confirm acceptance in writing +terms + basis of charging ○ To sol if instr by sol ○ To cl. If intsr by cl. ○ If BSB auth'd body get cl consent to disclose+give control of files to BSB or agent where terms of auth to practise not met [these terms not on syllabus] • No need to do it again re varied/additional instructions as deemed accepted on same terms as when you began the work, unless specified otherwise • Must comply with these 2 bullet points before doing the work Unless not reasonably practicable; so do it as soon as it is reasonably practicable.		

Intentionally Blank

Intentionally Blank

YOU AND YOUR CLIENT
Guidance fourth page

	(ii) (a)		(II) (B)

YOU AND YOUR CLIENT	Returning Instructions	<u>Cease to act and return</u> if
		
		○ Have started but any one of the 10 above re not accepting arises. PROMPTLY return
		
		○ Legal aid/crim funding wrongly obtained and cl does not remedy it immediately
		
		○ Cl refuses to allow you to disclose something to court
		
		○ Another is
		   ○ Become aware of doc should have been but was not disclosed
		   ○ You advise cl they need to disclose it and they don't/won't let you
			CD1
			CD2 [129]

		<u>MAY cease to act and return</u> if
		○ Your prof conduct called into question; OR
		
		○ Cl consents; OR
		
		○ You are self employed or a BSB authorised body
		PLUS
		○ Prof diary already has something in it where hearing on that date and reasonable efforts to prevent it OR
		○ Ill/pregnancy/childbirth/bereavement /similar prevents
		○ You are unavoidably on jury service
		
		• You are not paid when due
		
		• Aware, re what you are instructed on, of
		  ○ confidential docs/priv'd info
		  ○ docs of another
		
		• in litig +
		  ○ cl not consent to ceasing to act; or
		  ○ your application to come off the record has been granted
		
		• SOME OTHER SUBSTANTIAL REASON
			CD3

		All subject to
		• Getting cl consent or explain reason for ceasing to act to cl
		
		• Not being discrim re
		  ❖ It being objectionable to you/public
		  ❖ Cl conduct, opinions, beliefs, objectionable to you/public
		
		Source of finance properly to be given to prospective cl for the proceedings
			CD 8

---

[129] *CD2* has been added here because you sometimes need to state in an answer that there is no breach of *CD2* where what the client may see as in their best interests would mean a breach of Professional Ethics, e.g. **of** *CD1*. **IN THIS CASE YOU NEED TO EXPLAIN TO YOUR CLIENT THE "FRACTION" ½ IN** *column (iv)* of your Rubric Planning Template.

YOU AND YOUR CLIENT
Guidance fourth page

Column (ii)(c)

Intentionally Blank

YOU AND YOUR CLIENT
Rules, CDs and *Guidance fourth page* all on one page

	(ii) (a)	(II) (B)	(iii) (c)

	Returning Instructions	<u>Cease to act and return</u> *if*
		
		○ *Have started but any one of the 10 above re not accepting arises. PROMPTLY return*
		
		○ *Legal aid/crim funding wrongly obtained and cl does not remedy it immediately*
		
		○ *Cl refuses to allow you to disclose something to court*
		
		○ *Another is*
		   ○ *Become aware of doc should have been but was not disclosed*
		   ○ *You advise cl they need to disclose it and they don't/won't let you*
			CD1
			CD2 [130]	

		<u>MAY cease to act and return</u> *if* ○ *Your prof conduct called into question; OR* ○ *Cl consents; OR* ○ *You are self employed or a BSB authorised body* PLUS ○ *Prof diary already has something in it where hearing on that date and reasonable efforts to prevent it OR* ○ *Ill/pregnancy/childbirth/bereavement /similar prevents* ○ *You are unavoidably on jury service* • *You are not paid when due* • *Aware, re what you are instructed on, of* ○ *confidential docs/priv'd info* ○ *docs of another* • *in litig +* ○ *cl not consent to ceasing to act; or* ○ *your application to come off the record has been granted* • SOME OTHER SUBSTANTIAL REASON	*CD3*	
		All subject to • *Getting cl consent or explain reason for ceasing to act to cl* • *Not being discrim re* ❖ *It being objectionable to you/public* ❖ *Cl conduct, opinions, beliefs, objectionable to you/public* *Source of finance properly to be given to prospective cl for the proceedings*	*CD 8*	

---

[130] *CD2* has been added here because you sometimes need to state in an answer that there is no breach of *CD2* where what the client may see as in their best interests would mean a breach of Professional Ethics, e.g. of *CD1*. *IN THIS CASE YOU NEED TO EXPLAIN TO YOUR CLIENT THE "FRACTION" ½ IN* column (iv) of your Rubric Planning Template.

Once you have finished this book (2)

Activity

> In order to finish off Part C of the Handbook, the *Conduct Rules*, you now need to complete your learning of the *Rules* and *CDS* and *Guidance* for
>
> - *YOU AND YOUR REGULATOR* (Section C4) and
>
> - *YOU AND YOUR PRACTICE* (Section C5)
>
> [Space for doing this has not been included in this book]

Please do not be downhearted by the amount of time it has already taken to cover what we have in this book so far. There are two bits of good news.

1. Volume-wise, you have by now already covered at least half of the syllabus. The remainder of the syllabus is made up mostly of fairly short sections, compared to those you have already completed.

2. With what you have completed already, you would have been able to complete the whole of the Bar Standards Board's mock assessments for 2017 and 2018, apart from part of one question on each paper which required reference to one of ***Parts 2, 3 or 4 of the syllabus***.

Therefore the next item in this book is a new Question, Question N, for you to try your hand at.

Before you do, it may be an idea for you to either

- take photocopies of the pages of this book where you have completed the *Rules*, *CDs* and *Guidance* all on one page for

    - *YOU AND THE COURT*
    - *BEHAVING ETHICALLY*
    - *YOU AND YOUR CLIENT*; or

- take some time to type them out for yourself so that you are able to print copies,

    as in this way you can use them as templates when practising questions on these areas from your Provider. Constant use of the templates will go a very long way to making their contents stay in your brain.

You are now in a position to answer Question N[131]

There is no space in this book allotted for that.

You asked your client, Georgina Venables and your instructing solicitor to attend at conference with you last week. You are representing her in a case where she is being sued by one of the residents of one particular road in her area, known locally as 'Remoaner Road', for distributing leaflets in favour of Brexit, because he finds them offensive. His name is Tarquin Fotheringaye. You yourself voted 'leave' in the referendum. Mr Fotheringaye is alleging that Georgina must have stolen the door key from under a plant pot by his front door as that went missing on the day that the leaflet was delivered. He insists that it is quite distinctive as it is has a European Union flag painted on it on both sides. Georgina denies that she delivered any such leaflets and therefore also maintains that she did not steal the key.

She arrived for the conference late and very flustered. She insisted on emptying out her handbag to find a tissue and out of the bag fell a large bundle of leaflets stating 'Remoaners need to stop moaning'. She picked it up hurriedly and said,' You didn't see, that, right?' She then rushed out of the room in tears and her solicitor has persuaded her to come to see you again in a few days time. He does inform you, however, that Georgina will not allow you to mention in court the bundle of leaflets that both you and the solicitor clearly saw.

a) Giving full reasons, set out the issues you will need to address with Georgina when she next comes to see you, if at the outset, she continues to maintain the same position. **(6 marks).**

Today is now the day that the next meeting is due to take place. The solicitor has just telephoned you to say that Georgina has agreed that any issues in last week's meeting should be dealt with in the way that you advised her solicitor. She still maintains that she did not deliver any leaflets. The solicitor also tells you that Tarquin Fotheringaye is going to be representing himself. Mr Fotheringaye has no professional qualifications. During the phone call, the solicitor asked you if you saw the newly reported case yesterday. The decision was that a person distributing political leaflets without a licence lost his case [132]. You had been planning to use as your strongest argument for Georgina that a licence is not necessary for distributing her leaflets. The solicitor also tells you that he is of the opinion that you should not raise the new reported case when you get to court, as Georgina has a better chance of being acquitted if you don't. You reply that you will call him back in a few minutes once you have considered the ethics of his suggestion.

b) Explain what you will say to the solicitor when you call him back, as to whether or not you will raise the newly reported case in court. **(4 marks).**

---

[131] Please be aware that this question and suggested mark scheme have not been through the rigorous processes that that will be the case for the actual assessment questions. They are, though, as close a representation as possible for illustrative purposes, of assessment questions and mark schemes.

[132] As far as the author is aware in real life there is no such newly reported case. This has been made up purely for Question N. The author has never seen this happen in a real assessment.

Intentionally Blank

Themes

You will have noticed from references in the footnotes, that there are themes beginning to emerge from the pages of the Handbook. The way that the Handbook is set out, however, does not necessarily group all these themes together.

Therefore, the beginnings of grouping themes together appear next in this book. You will need to add to them as and when more themes develop from the syllabus, as well as adding further mentions of these initial themes whenever they arise again somewhere else in the syllabus.

CONFIDENTIALITY

Ethical issue	**Umbrella Heading of Handbook** [133]	*Rules* in the Handbook	Associated *CDS*	Any *CS*?
Confidentiality	You and the court	6/1 (put at end if ceasing to act and returning instructions)	*1* *6*	

	You and your client	• Keep client affairs confidential
		• Protect confidentiality of each client except
		  ○ Required/permitted by law
		  ○ Client gives informed consent
		• 4 of the 10 "Nos" re accepting = cannot accept where confidentiality to other clients means you cannot act in the interests of a prospective client, unless other client consents
		• Returning instructions – may if aware of confidential or private information, or docs belonging to another re what you are instructed on
			6
			
			6
			
			6
			
			2
			
			3
				42-45

---

[133] Remember that on the mark schemes that the author used for the assessments, there were no marks available in the assessment for including these 'umbrella terms' in your answers.

Themes

NOT DISCRIMINATING

Ethical issue	Umbrella Heading of Handbook [134]	*Rules* in the Handbook	Associated *CDS*	Any *CS*?
Not Discriminating	Behaving ethically	• Must not victimise or harass re anything	*3* - integrity	

	You and your client	• Returning instructions
		  ○ Must not discriminate
		    ▪ As what they say is objectionable to you/public
		    ▪ As what they do is objectionable to you/public
		    ▪ Re the source of finance to be given to the client
		• 'cab-rank' rule		

---

[134] Remember that on the mark schemes that the author used for the assessments, there were no marks available in the assessment for including these 'umbrella terms' in your answers.

INDEPENDENCE

Ethical issue	Umbrella Heading of Handbook [135]	*Rules* in the Handbook	Associated *CDS*	Any *CS*?
Independence	You and the court	- Independence in the interests of justice o Ensure independence is not compromised	4	
	Behaving ethically	- [Honesty, integrity and] independence o Do not undermine it	4	Would gift mean others think you are not independent?

	You and your client	- 4/2
		
		- Personal responsibility
		  o Use your own professional judgment to be able to justify decisions and actions, notwithstanding the views of others
		- Accepting instructions
		  o 10 of the 10 "Nos" re accepting = cannot accept if real prospect you are not able to maintain your independence
			4
			2
			
			4
			
			4	

---

[135] Remember that on the mark schemes that the author used for the assessments, there were no marks available in the assessment for including these 'umbrella terms' in your answers.

Themes

NOT MISLEADING

Ethical issue	Umbrella Heading of Handbook [136]	*Rules* in the Handbook	Associated *CDS*	Any *CCs*?
Not Misleading	You and the court	• Must not mislead the **court** 　o No untrue/misleading submissions/questions 　o Can call W re untrue/misleading if you tell the court	*1*	
	Behaving ethically	• Must not (attempt to) mislead **anyone**	*3*	
	You and your client	• Not misleading clients or potential clients[137] 　o When offering/supplying[138] legal services, re 　　▪ Scope of services 　　▪ Terms/who basis of charging 　　▪ Who legally responsible 　　▪ Entitled to perform/regulated 　　▪ Any insurance for Prof Neg		

---

[136] Remember that on the mark schemes that the author used for the assessments, there were no marks available in the assessment for including these 'umbrella terms' in your answers.

[137] See (see also D6 in area 1 of syllabus, part 2 of the Handbook)

[138] Remember to tie this in with area D6 of the syllabus

THINK LIKE AN EXAMINER

Now that you are conversant with

- the workings of the Handbook
- possible mark schemes
- planning and answering techniques using a Rubric Planning Template and Templates; and
- the existence of themes throughout the syllabus

you may now feel empowered to start thinking like an examiner as you confront the rest of your Professional Ethics course and revision.

The author would posit that you could now pick any element of the syllabus that you would like to 'test', (or revise) then all you need to do is make sure that

- the themes follow through in your suggested answer
- you include all relevant *Rules*, *CORE DUTIES* and *Guidance* in the Handbook in your suggested answer
- you remember to refer also any relevant parts of ***the other areas of the syllabus (i.e. Areas 2, 3 and 4)*** too; and
- you build a scenario remembering that, as you have seen, it is perfectly possible for a question to be created which requires in its answer
  - only the Handbook (***Area 1*** of the syllabus); yet also a question could be created which requires in its answer
  - only ***Area 2*** or ***Area 3*** or ***Area 4*** of the syllabus; or
  - a mix of [any feasible] combination of ***Area 1, Area 2, Area 3 or Area 4*** of the syllabus.

For the sake of practice during revision, you could also take scenarios you have already come across and change one or two of the facts, to get a different answer.

For example, remember how for Question A, different ethical rules came into play regarding whether it was the lay client or the solicitor who is trying to persuade you to act outside the ambit of the ethical rules.

There will be some more examples after you have answered Question N later on.

Intentionally Blank

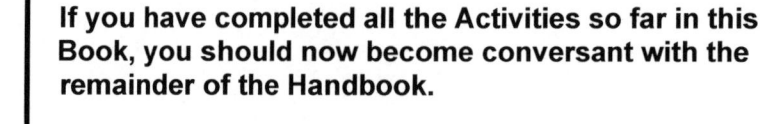

Once you have finished this book (3)

> **Activity**
>
> **If you have completed all the Activities so far in this Book, you should now become conversant with the remainder of the Handbook.**
>
> **If you have bought into the idea of incremental learning then you should begin with the *Rules* and associated *CDS* in**
>
> - **Part 3 of the Handbook -   B2, B3, B7 & B9   C1 & C2**
>
> - **Part 4 of the Handbook -   B8 C – rQ130-135**
>
> [Part 6 of the Handbook, the definitions section will not be discretely examined, but knowledge of the Handbook's definitions relevant to the rest of the syllabus is required.]
>
> - **The Equality Rules**

> **Activity**
>
> All (!) – it's not too much – that remains for you assimilate are
>
> *Areas 2, 3 and 4 of the syllabus*
>
> - Area 2 is Code Guidance
>   - Guidance on Practising Rules and Requirements
>   - Guidance on the Administration of a Barrister's Practice,
>   - Guidance on the Professional Conduct of Barristers,
>   - Additional Guidance;
>
> - Area 3 is Crown Prosecution Service Publications; and
>
> - Area 4 is Money Laundering and terrorist financing.
>
> Please refer back to the section of this book on the syllabus for a further breakdown of each of these parts.
>
> **and then**
>
> devise a system of mapping each of *Areas 2, 3 and 4* onto Part 1 of the syllabus, the Handbook. That can save valuable time in the assessment.

Once you have finished this book (3)

Answering Question N (a)

Here are the workings for Question N which was set out a few pages ago.

Question N (a)

First Issue = Leaflet - She refuses to let me disclose the existence of a document.

Second Issue = Key - I need to address the matter of the key.

First, identify the relevant areas.

Section C - The Conduct Rules

YOU AND THE COURT

BEHAVING ETHICALLY

YOU AND YOUR CLIENT

YOU AND YOUR REGULATOR

YOU AND YOUR PRACTICE
   ↓

The Conduct Rules

YOU AND THE COURT

- *Independence in the interests of justice*
- *Not misleading the court*
- ~~*Not abusing your role as an advocate*~~

~~*BEHAVING ETHICALLY*~~

- ~~*Honesty, integrity and independence*~~
- ~~*Referral fees*~~
- ~~*Undertakings*~~
- ~~*Discrimination*~~
- ~~*Foreign work*~~

YOU AND YOUR CLIENT

1. *Best interests of each client, provision of a competent standard of work and confidentiality*
2. ~~*Not misleading potential clients (see also D6 in area 1 of syllabus, part 2 of the Handbook)*~~
3. *Personal responsibility*
8. ~~*The 'cab-rank' rule*~~[139]
4. *Accepting Instructions*
5. ~~*Defining terms or basis on which instructions are accepted*~~
6. *Returning instructions*
7. ~~*Requirement not to discriminate*~~

---

[139] Remember that this numbering sequence is correct, as we have chosen to deal with the *'cab-rank' rule* before Accepting Instructions.

The next pages show the above recall
expanded into the "all on one page"
YOU AND THE COURT
YOU AND YOUR CLIENT
Rubric Planning Templates
which were set out earlier in this book.

Answering Question N (a)

YOU AND THE COURT

	(ii) (a)		(II) (B)	(III) (C)
~~YOU AND THE COURT~~	Independence in the interests of justice	• Not mislead • ~~Not abuse role~~ [140] • Not waste court time • ~~Ensure decisions and law~~ • Indep not comp	CD4	~~CC4~~ ~~CC5,9,13~~
	CD1/CD2		CD1 CD2	~~CC6~~ ~~CC8, 9,11, 12,14~~
	CD6/CD1		CD6	~~CC8,9,13~~
	Not mislead the court	Includes • No untrue/misleading submissions or questions • ~~Can call W re untrue/misleading if you tell the court~~		~~CC7,9,10~~

	~~Not abusing your role as an advocate~~	~~Includes~~
		• ~~Not insult anyone~~
		• ~~Only make serious alleg v W if they've had a chance to answer you in XX~~
		• ~~Not accuse other re your cl's crime without~~
		   ○ ~~Reasonable grounds +~~
		   ○ ~~Rel to cl's case or W credibility +~~
		   ○ ~~Not name 3rd pty in open ct unless reasonably nec~~
		• ~~Not give own opinion unless ct/law asks~~
			~~CD3 + CD5~~	

---

[140] Those elements of the Rubric Planning Template which are not relevant for answering Question N are faded. They are also crossed out.

Answering Question N (a)

Answering Question N (a)

YOU AND YOUR CLIENT

YOU AND YOUR CLIENT	• Best interests of each [141] client	~~Best interests duty includes if cl best served by different legal rep + inform cl of this~~	CD2	~~gC8~~
	• Competent standard of work and service	~~This incl duty to tell (sol/lay) cl asap if~~ ~~— Apparent can't do it in time / in reasonable time~~ ~~— any risk of this~~	CD7	

	• Confidentiality	~~All 3 can be read to include~~
		• ~~Fearlessly and lawfully promote cl's best interests~~
		• ~~No regard to own interests / consequences — mitigate any breach~~
		• ~~No regard to consequences for others~~
		• ~~Not allow anyone to limit yr discretion re serving clients' interests~~
		• Protect the confidentiality of each cl except
		  ○ Req'd/permitted by law
		  ○ Cl gives informed consent
			CD6
			
			6/1 "FRACTION"
			
			CD1
			CD2
			~~CD3~~
			~~CD4~~
			
			~~CD8/CD2~~
				~~gC42~~
				
				~~gC13~~
				
				C43

	CD 1/2 ~~CD 3/2~~ ~~CD 4/2~~ ~~Guidance also adds in CD8/CD2~~			
	~~Not misleading clients or potential clients~~	~~Not mislead/cause/permit who you supply to/offer to re~~ • ~~Nature and scope of legal services~~ • ~~Terms/who do it/basis of charging~~ • ~~Who legally responsible~~ • ~~Entitled to perform/regulated~~ • ~~Any insurance for Prof Neg~~ [142]	~~CD3~~ ~~CD5~~	

---

[141] So you need to consider both clients if there are two of them. Considering the interests of EACH
[142] Personal responsibility and the 'cab-rank' rule are not relevant to this question and so have been omitted to save space.

Answering Question N (a)

	(ii)	(a)	(II)	(B)	(III)	(C)
YOU AND YOUR CLIENT	Accepting Instructions	• No if 1 2 3 4 5 instructions seem limit authority/discretion in court 6 instructions need you to act illegally/against the Handbook 7 8 9 10	CD1 CD4			
	~~Defining terms or basis on which instructions are accepted~~	• ~~Confirm acceptance in writing + terms + basis of charging~~ ~~– To sol if instr by sol~~ ~~– To cl if instr by cl.~~ ~~– If BSB auth'd body get cl consent to disclose + give control of files to BSB or agent where terms of auth to practise not met~~ ~~[these terms not on syllabus]~~ • ~~No need to do it again re varied/additional instructions as deemed accepted on same terms as when you began the work, unless specified otherwise~~ • ~~Must comply with these 2 bullet points before doing the work~~ ~~Unless~~ ~~not reasonably practicable: so do it as soon as it is reasonably practicable.~~			

192

Answering Question N (a)

(ii)	(a)	(II) (B)	(iii) (c)

~~YOU AND YOUR CLIENT~~	*Returning Instructions*	<u>Cease to act and return</u> if
		
		○ Have started but any one of the 10 above re not accepting arises. PROMPTLY return
		
		~~○ Legal aid/crim funding wrongly obtained and cl does not remedy it immediately~~
		
		○ Cl refuses to allow you to disclose something to court
		
		○ Another is
		   ○ Become aware of doc should have been but was not disclosed
		   ○ You advise cl they need to disclose it and they don't/won't let you
			CD1
			CD2 [143]
				~~cC11~~
				
				~~c13~~

		~~MAY cease to act and return if~~ ~~○ Your prof conduct called into question; OR~~ ~~○ Cl consents; OR~~ ~~○ You are self employed or a BSB authorised body~~ ~~PLUS~~ ~~○ Prof diary already has something in it where hearing on that date and reasonable efforts to prevent it OR~~ ~~○ Ill/pregnancy/childbirth/bereavement /similar prevents~~ ~~○ You are unavoidably on jury service~~ ~~● You are not paid when due~~ ~~● Aware, re what you are instructed on, of~~ ~~○ confidential docs/priv'd info~~ ~~○ docs of another~~ ~~● in litig +~~ ~~○ cl not consent to ceasing to act or~~ ~~○ your application to come off the record has been granted~~ ~~● SOME OTHER SUBSTANTIAL REASON~~	~~CD3~~	
		All subject to ● Getting cl consent or explain reason for ceasing to act to cl ~~● Not being discrim re~~ ~~○ It being objectionable to you/public~~ ~~○ Cl conduct, opinions, beliefs, objectionable to you/public~~ ~~Source of finance properly to be given to prospective cl for the proceedings~~	~~CD8~~	

Next a reminder of the Rubric Planning Template Headings.

---

[143] CD2 has been added here because you sometimes need to state in an answer that there is no breach of CD2 where what the client may see as in their best interests would mean a breach of Professional Ethics, e.g. of CD1. **IN THIS CASE YOU NEED TO EXPLAIN TO YOUR CLIENT THE "FRACTION" ½ IN** ~~*column (iv)*~~ of your Rubric Planning Template.

Answering Question N (a)

Answering Question N (a)

Identify the Issue	**D**escribe the relevant parts of the syllabus	**E**xplain with reference to the contents of the scenario	*Advise resolve*

(i) Identify ethical issues. State them generically	(ii) set out the relevant bits of the syllabus i.e.
	• **Syllabus Area 1;**
	  ○ Relevant parts of the Handbook –
	    ○ Part 1, 2, 3, 4 or 6?
	    ○ Equality Rules?
	any of syllabus Areas 2, 3 and 4?
		(iii) apply your knowledge with a reasoned explanation of breach/no breach	(iv) *Resolve i.e. advise*[144]

(i) Identify ethical issues. State them generically [145]	(ii) set out the relevant bits of the syllabus i.e. • Conduct rules (rC) (ii)(a) YOU AND THE COURT YOU AND YOUR CLIENT • RELEVANT CDS(II)(B) • *relevant guidance (gC) (II)(c)*	(iii) apply your knowledge with a reasoned explanation of breach/no breach	(iv) *Resolve i.e. advise*
Question N			
a) set out the issues you will need to address with Georgina when she next comes to see you, if at the outset, she continues to maintain the same position about the leaflet.		Giving full reasons,	
First ethical issue Leaflets			
Second Issue Key			

For the remainder of Question N a) we are going to put columns *(i), (ii)(a), (ii)(b)* and *(ii)(c)* on the lefthand pages and then all columns including *(iii)* and *(iv)* on the righthand pages.

195

Answering Question N (a)

Column (i)	Column (ii) (a)	COLUMN (II)(B)	Column (II) (C)
First issue Leaflets *Lay client refuses to allow me to disclose a document*	Independence in the interests of justice • Not mislead • Not waste court time CD1/CD2 CD6/CD1	CD4 CD1 CD2 CD6 CD1	rC5, rC9,
	Not mislead the court Includes • No untrue/misleading submissions or questions		

	• Best interests of each client
	
	• Competent standard of work and service
	
	• Confidentiality
	• Protect the confidentiality of each cl except
	  ○ Req'd/permitted by law
	  ○ Cl gives informed consent
		CD2
		
		CD7
		
		CD6
		
		6/1 "FRACTION"
			rC8
			
			rC42
			rC13
			
			rC43

196

Answering Question N (a)

(i)	(ii) (a), (ii) (b) and (ii) (c)	(iii)	(iv)
First issue Leaflets *Lay client refuses to allow me to disclose a document*	Independence in the interests of justice CD4 • ~~Not mislead~~ SEE BELOW • ~~Not waste court time~~ gC9 this fits better at the end of column (iv) for this question ~~CD1/CD2~~ fits better with bests interests of each client below ~~CD6/CD1~~ moved to end column (iv)	*I and sol saw leaflets fall out of her bag, stating that Remoaners need to stop moaning. These are documents that must be disclosed even though it adversely affects her case. If I do not disclose the leaflet as she will not allow me to, I would be influenced by her and would be breaching the rule in the handbook on the code of practice as I would not be acting independently.*[146]	*Explain this to Georgina*
	Not mislead the court Includes No untrue/misleading submissions or questions CD 1	*Not disclosing the leaflet in court would be a breach of this rule.* *Misleading the court in this way would be a breach of CD1*	*Explain this to her*
	• Best interests of each client CD2 ~~gC8~~ gC8 fits better at end column (iv) • Competent standard of work and service CD 7 ~~Confidentiality CD 6~~ ~~gC42~~ ~~Protect the confidentiality of gC43 each cl except~~ ◦ ~~Req'd/permitted by law CD6/CD1 C43~~ ◦ ~~Cl gives informed consent~~ Moved to end column (iv)	*Georgina would doubtless argue that I would be in breach of CD2 and not acting in her best interests if I advise her to allow me to disclose the document.*	*Tell her my duty to the court overrides my duty to act in the best interests of each client. This I would not be in breach by advising her to allow me to disclose the leaflet. For same reason I would not be breach of providing her with a competent standard of work and service.*

---

[146] Remember that independence is more likely to arise when there is a possible conflict of interests

Answering Question N (a)

Column (i)	Column (ii) (a)	COLUMN (II)(B)	Column (II) (C)
First issue Leaflets *Lay client refuses to allow me to disclose a document*	Independence in the interests of justice		
	Not mislead the ocurt		
	Best interests etc		

	Accepting Instructions
	• No if
	   instructions seem to limit authority/discretion in court
	
	   instructions need you to act illegally/against the Handbook
		CD1
		CD4	

	Returning Instructions
	<u>Cease to act and return</u> if
	
	○ Have started but any one of the 10 above re not accepting arises. PROMPTLY return
	
	○ Cl refuses to allow you to disclose something to court
	
	○ Another is
	  ○ Become aware of doc should have been but was not disclosed
	  ○ You advise cl they need to disclose it and they don't/won't let you
		CD1
		CD2
			rC11
			
			r13

	All subject to • Getting cl consent or explain reason for ceasing to act to cl		
Second Issue Key			

198

Answering Question N (a)

(i)	(ii) (a), (ii) (b) and (ii) (c)	(iii)	(iv)
First issue Leaflets *Lay client refuses to allow me to disclose a document*	*Accepting Instructions* • *No if instructions seem to limit authority/discretion in court CD1 CD4* *instructions need you to act illegally/against the Handbook*[147]	*Since not allowing me to disclose the leaflet limits my authority/discretion in court and since not allowing me to disclose it puts me in breach of provisions of the handbook as above, Georgina is in effect asking me to act against the handbook.*	
	Returning Instructions *Cease to act and return if* ○ *Have started but any one of the 10 above re not accepting arises. PROMPTLY return* **ADD IN THE 2 ABOVE INTO HERE** *Cl refuses to allow you to disclose something to court CD1 CD2 gC11* ○ *Another is Become aware of doc should have been but was not disclosed [g13 is already in column (iv)* *You advise cl they need to disclose it and they don't/won't let you*		*Must PROMPTLY return if she continues to refuse to allow me to disclose the leaflet after I have explained to her why I should disclose.* *Explain to her*
	All subject to • *Getting cl consent or explain reason for ceasing to act to cl*		*Must not cease to act and return instructions without either client consent or explaining reason.*
			Not waste court time gC9 *Confidentiality CD6 gC42* *Protect the confidentiality of gC43* *each cl except* ○ *Req'd/permitted by law CD6/CD1 gC43*[148] *gC8* ○ *Cl gives informed consent* *Tell client re 6/1*

---

[147] If returning instructions for 'one of the 10' of *rC21* it makes sense to deal with returning first then feeding in which of the 10 are relevant.

[148] Since 6/1 will need to addressed following return of instructions, yet where you knew of something confidential about your client, it works better if you move this to the very end of *column (iv)* as the place to address it in your answer.

			She will have to fin another barrister. I won't tell him or the court about the leaflet.
Second Issue – Key [149] *Need to address this with her and the solicitor.*			Ask Georgina again what her position is regarding the key.

---

[149] Be honest – did you remember to address this in your answer? For now, it was there only to drive home the point about the need to answer the question fully.

Answering Question N (a)

Question N(a), a mark scheme [150]

- *Lay client refuses to allow me to disclose a document.*

  - There is a rule in the Handbook that Barristers owe a duty to the court to act with independence in the interests of justice. (½) Also Core Duty 4 states that "You must maintain your independence." (½) [It may be that you only get these marks if you have applied them as in the next paragraphs].

    I and the solicitor saw a leaflet fall out of her bag, stating that Remoaners need to stop moaning. (½) This is a document that must be disclosed even though it adversely affects her case.

    If I do not disclose the leaflet as she will not allow me to, I would be influenced by her and would be breaching the rule in the handbook on the code of practice as I would not be acting independently in the interests of justice. (½)

    This is one thing I will need to explain to Georgina.

  - By another rule I must not mislead the court. This includes that must make no untrue or misleading submissions or ask untrue or misleading questions. (½) [It may be that you only get these marks if you have applied them as in the next paragraph].

    Not disclosing the leaflet in court would be a breach of this rule as it would necessitate such submissions or questions. (½) It would also be a breach of Core Duty 1 which states, "You must observe your duty to the court in the administration of justice." (½)

    This is another thing I will need to explain to Georgina.

  - CD2 states that, "You must act in the best interests of each client". (½) There is also a rule to this effect.
  - CD7 states that, "You must provide a competent standard of work and service to each client." (½) There is also a rule which says this. [It may be that you only get these marks if you have applied them as in the next paragraph].

    Georgina would doubtless argue that I would be in breach of CD2 and CD7 and not acting in her best interests and not giving her a competent standard of work and service if I advise her to allow me to disclose the document. (½ for either of these – maximum ½)

    I will tell Georgina that my duty to the court overrides my duty to act in the best interests of each client. (½) Thus I would not be in breach in advising her to allow me to disclose the leaflet. For the same reason I would not be breach of providing her with a competent standard of work and service.

  - Another rule in the Handbook says that I must return instructions, ceasing to act if the client's instructions seem to limit my authority or discretion in court, (½) or if the instructions need me to act outside the rules of the Handbook. (½) The same is the case if a client refuses to allow to disclose something to the court. (½) Guidance in the Handbook shows that if I would mislead the court unless I disclosed a confidential document, I should ask the client's permission to disclose. If that permission is refused, I should cease to act and return my instructions and I will not reveal that information to the court. (½) [It may be that you only get these marks if you have applied them as in the next paragraph].

---

[150] Please be aware that this question and suggested mark scheme have not been through the rigorous processes that that will be the case for the actual assessment questions. They are, though, as close a representation as possible for illustrative purposes, of assessment questions and mark schemes.

Answering Question N (a)

- Since not allowing me to disclose the leaflet limits my authority/discretion in court and since not allowing me to disclose it puts me in breach of provisions of the handbook, Georgina is in effect asking me to act against the handbook. (½)

I will explain to Georgina that I must PROMPTLY return her instructions if she continues to refuse to allow me to disclose the leaflets after I have explained to her why I should disclose. (½) I could also add that another rule with the same result, is that should I become aware of a document that should have been disclosed but has not been and the client will not allow me to do so. (½) (maximum of ½ for this paragraph)

- Another rule is that before returning instructions a barrister needs either the consent of the client or needs to explain the reason for ceasing to act to the client. (½) [It may be that you only get these marks if you have applied them as in the next paragraph].

- If Georgina continues to maintain the same position about the leaflet, and if she will not give her consent to me ceasing to act, I will not be in breach of this rule as I will have explained the above reasons to her. (½)

- In relation to the rule about not wasting court time, there is guidance to the effect that when ceasing to act for the above reasons, a barrister cannot reveal the contents of the document to the court. (½) This chimes with CD6 which states, "You must keep the affairs of each client confidential". (½) Other guidance sets out that this CD is central to the administration of justice. [It may be that you only get these marks if you have applied them as in the next paragraph]

- A barrister must protect the confidentiality of each client except where disclosures are required or permitted by law or to which the client gives informed consent. (½) CD6 states that, "You must keep the affairs of each client confidential." (½) Another rule sets out that keeping client affairs confidential is not in breach of the duty to the court. (½)

I will explain to Georgina that on returning the instructions, I am duty bound not to reveal the existence of the Remoaners leaflet so that I will not tell the court or any future lawyer she instructs on this matter. (½)

The Key (say 3 x (½))

Think like an examiner - Notice how in this scenario N, that you are told that your persuasions and beliefs are the same as your clients. What ethical issues arise in situations where your personal moral compass, opinions or beliefs are directly contrary to those of your client? (YOU AND THE COURT, BEHAVING ETHICALLY, YOU AND YOUR CLIENT all have elements of them that are pertinent here).

Think like an examiner – remember to take questions that you have been asked on your course and then change or embellish them for extra practice. Here, for example, what if the office cleaner leaves a European Union key found on the floor of your office on your template? What if you raise this with Georgina, believing it could well have fallen out of her bag when she was looking for a tissue and the leaflet fell out? What if she denies any knowledge of the key but you don't believe her. Could you continue to represent her? (See *Guidance* on YOU AND THE COURT)

Intentionally Blank

The final Rubric Planning Template for this book

Following on from the possible mark scheme for Question N (a), the Rubric Planning Template is now reproduced and embellished on this page to include some stylistic hints and tips that you may find it useful to employ when answering questions. These are

1. When referring to *CD6 AND THE "FRACTION" 6/1* the best place for it in your answer is at the end, as it is what you will explain to your client, should you need to advise them about the consequences of returning instructions.

2. Trying to find the words to introduce *CD2* and associated rules can be a little elusive. We found that the words "Your client may say that you are not working in their best interests....." This then allows you to counter with the "fraction" *CD1/CD2*.

3. *gCs* need to be included for an outstanding answer. Notice, though, how, often, they simply reinforce what the *rules* have said. The first notable example of when they go further than the *rules* is in *gCs 18-20* on gifts.

*I*dentify the Issue	*D*escribe the relevant parts of the syllabus	*E*xplain with reference to the contents of the scenario	*A*dvise resolve

(i) Identify ethical issues. State them generically	**(ii) set out the relevant bits of the syllabus i.e.**
	• **Syllabus Area 1;**
	  ○ Relevant parts of the Handbook
	  ○ Area 2, 3, 4 or 6 ?
	  ○ Equality Rules?
	
	(ii)(a)= rules
	
	(ii)(b)= CDS
	
	(ii)(c)= gCs
	
	gCs often reinforce,
	
	yet 18-20 on gifts.
	
	(ii)(d)=
	• *Any of syllabus Areas 2, 3 and 4?*
		(iii) apply your knowledge with a reasoned explanation of breach/no breach
		
		Column (iii) Relate back to column (i) but putting in the actual facts of the scenario, lift words from the scenario and the question.
		
		• *CD2 "CLIENT MAY SAY..." BARRISTER EXPLAINS 1/2*
			(iv) Resolve i.e. advise
			
			• *6/1 AT END*

205

Intentionally Blank

Answering Question N (b)

Question N (b), planning and a possible mark scheme [151]

o *Issue - Solicitor suggests I do not mention the new case.*

Relevant areas of the syllabus

YOU AND THE COURT ⟶

YOU AND YOUR CLIENT ⟶

Rubric Planning Template headings amended to become the start of your Rubric Planning Template for Question N (b)

Identify the Issue	*Describe* the relevant parts of the syllabus	*Explain* with reference to the contents of the scenario	*Advise* resolve

(i) Identify ethical issues. State them generically	(ii) set out the relevant bits of the syllabus i.e.
	• Syllabus Area 1;
	  o Relevant parts of the Handbook
	  o Area 1, 2, 3, 4 or 5?
	
	 ~~Equality Rules?~~
	
	 (ii)(a)= rules
	
	 (ii)(B)= CDS
	
	 ~~(ii)(c)= SCs~~
	
	 ~~SCs often reinforce,~~
	 ~~ref~~
	 ~~18-20 on gifts.~~
	
	 ~~(ii)(d)=~~
	• ~~Any of syllabus Parts 2, 3 and 4?~~
		(iii) apply your knowledge with a reasoned explanation of breach/no breach
		
		 Column (iii) Relate back to column (i) but putting in the actual facts of the scenario, lift words from the scenario and the question.
		 CD2 "CLIENT MAY SAY…"
		 BARRISTER EXPLAINS 1/2
			(iv) Resolve i.e. advise
			
			 ~~6/1 at end~~

	as to whether or not you will raise the newly reported case in court		*Explain what you will say to the solicitor when you call him back*

---

[151] Please be aware that this question and suggested mark scheme have not been through the rigorous processes that that will be the case for the actual assessment questions. They are, though, as close a representation as possible for illustrative purposes, of assessment questions and mark schemes.

Answering Question N (b)

Recalling and identifying the relevant parts of the syllabus

First, columns *(ii)(a)*, *(ii)(b)* and *(ii)(c)*

~~YOU AND THE COURT~~ [152]	*(ii)(a)* Independence in the interests of justice CD1/CD2	*(ii)(a)* • Not waste court time • Ensure decisions and law • Indep not comp	*(ii)(b)* CD4 CD1 CD2	*(ii)(c)* ~~rC5.~~
~~YOU AND YOUR CLIENT~~	*Personal Responsibility*	*Notwithstanding views of others, use own prof judgment be able to justify decisions and actions*	CD4	~~rC26.~~

and then all columns including *(i)*, (ii) - *(ii)(a)*, *(ii)(b)* and *(ii)(c)*, *(iii)* and *(iv)* after that.

---

[152] Crossed out as you get no marks for saying this

Answering Question N (b)

(i)	(ii)	(iii)	(iv)
Solicitor suggests I do not mention the new case.	*Independence in the interests of justice* **CD4** • *Not waste court time* **gC5.** • *Ensure decisions and law* • *Indep not comp* **CD1/CD2**	*would be if argued without ref to new case law* *Positive duty.* *Would be breach if I didn't* **CD2 "CLIENT MAY SAY..." B EXPLAINS 1/2** **CD2 SOL HAS SAID** *G has a better chance of being acquitted if I don't. He may say that I would be in breach of CD2 otherwise.*	tell him about rule and CD and gc5 (TF is representing himself) ditto explain to him 1/2
	Personal Responsibility Notwithstanding views of others, use own prof judgment be able to justify decisions and actions **CD4**	*My own prof judgment tells me that in view of ensure decisions and law, CD1/2 and 4*	Tell him I must ensure the recent case is before the court, advise him that At today's meeting I will be telling G that there is a new case which changes what our arguments were going to be regarding the distributing of leaflets.

209

Answering Question N (b)

Answering Question N (b)

Question N (b) a possible mark scheme

- There is a rule in the Handbook that Barristers owe a duty to the court to act with independence in the interests of justice. (½) Also Core Duty 4 states that "You must maintain your independence." (½) [It may be that you only get these marks if you have applied them as in the next paragraphs].

    I would be in breach of both the rule and the CD if I blindly listened to him and simply agreed not to mention the new case in which a person distributing political leaflets without a licence lost his case. (½)

    I will tell the solicitor the content of this rule and CD explaining that I must maintain my independence in the interests of justice. Thus I will make my own decision as to how to deal with this new case. (½)

- There is a rule that a barrister must not waste court time. (½) Guidance to this rule says that a barrister must draw the court's attention to any decision adverse to the client's case and that this is especially important if acting against someone who is not legally represented. (½)

    The separate rule that a barrister must ensure that all relevant decisions and law are before the court further reinforces this. (½) [It may be that you only get these marks if you have applied them as in the next paragraphs].

    I would be in breach if I did not draw the court's attention to the new case where it was decided that a person does need a licence to distribute political leaflets. This is because the court would otherwise not have the latest legal decisions before it. (½)

    I would tell the solicitor that I will not waste the court's time by not setting the latest legal decisions before it and that this is even more necessary to see that justice is done as TF has no professional legal qualifications and is representing himself without the aid of a lawyer. (½)

- CD2 states that "you must act in the best interests of each client." (½) [It may be that you only get these marks if you have applied them as in the next paragraphs].

    When the solicitor opined that the new case should not be mentioned, as G has a better chance of being acquitted if I don't, he was effectively saying that I would otherwise be in breach of CD2. (½)

    I would explain to him that CD1 states that "you must observe your duty to the court in the administration of justice" and that the rules clearly set out that this duty overrides CD2. Therefore I would not be in breach of a rule or CD for not acting in Georgina's best interests. (½)

- Personal Responsibility remains with each barrister, and notwithstanding the views of others this rule goes on to say that a barrister must use his/her own professional judgment to be able to justify decisions and actions. (½) [It may be that you only get these marks if you have applied them as in the next paragraphs].

    Despite the solicitor's opinion that I should not mention the case to better help our client, I should tell the solicitor that I must ensure the recent case is before the court. I will also tell him that at today's meeting I will be telling G that there is a new case which changes what our arguments were going to be regarding the distributing of leaflets, so that we need to reappraise how to run this case. (½)

One query that students often had after final revision was,

"What if I did a full answer to a question, but the parts of the syllabus I used are not on the mark scheme?"

Either, you have made some kind of error and if that is the case, all you can do is wait to see how that affects your final mark;

Or, the best assurances I can give to that, are that for the real assessment, you will have noticed from some footnotes in this book, the questions and mark schemes have gone through a rigorous quality assurance process. Then, at every point during the marking process, markers flag up for further consideration any individual scripts that they feel need further consideration for whatever reason. This is in addition to the second marking that happens as a matter of course. It is usual that all involved in the examining and marking process will reconsider the mark schemes and where necessary the examiners will revise them at any point before the results are finalised.

The examiners and markers are really working full on between the assessment and the release of results. It is not in order to torture candidates that there seems to be such a long wait until the results are released. So much is going on in the process that candidates are unaware of during this period.

Preparing fully for this assessment is key. Preparing fully before you write your assessment answer is key.

I hope you find the key to your success.

Gillian Woodworth

Warmest wishes to all those sitting the Bar Professional Training Course or the Bar Transfer Test assessments in 2020.

Gillian Woodworth

November 2019

Printed in Great Britain
by Amazon